FLAYVAFUL

FLAYVAFUL

SPICE UP
YOUR KITCHEN!

**NATHANIEL
SMITH**

—

**THE
GRUBWORKS
KITCHEN**

Photography by Steven Joyce

murdoch books
London | Sydney

CONTENTS

FLAYVAFUL, IT'S HERE!

IT'S NO LONGER JUST AN IDEA. I could easily say I've thought about this day for as long as I can remember, but I honestly never thought I would have my own cookbook! A WHOLE BOOK. And not just any book, but a recipe book. This is definitely a pinch me moment.

As a chef who didn't go down the traditional route, I've always wanted to make food fun, but with flayvas! So as you work your way through these chapters, I hope you really get to experience a journey with food that brings you great joy, but most importantly I hope that your confidence continues to blossom to great heights. Don't be so hard on yourself either, don't take the fun out of cooking. It's okay if you make a mistake or accidentally miss a step, the world isn't going to end! The dish isn't going to be ruined. Will it taste different? Maybe, but it won't be bad. I hate to sound like a guru, but you cannot learn without making mistakes in the kitchen. I still make mistakes, I'm EXTREMELY clumsy, so don't worry, we're all in this together. As someone who was a rookie in the kitchen, I used to see Michelin–star–trained chefs sometimes get it wrong, so don't be hard on yourself.

Enjoy each chapter as it goes by, pick out your favourite recipes and make tweaks, then show off your new skills to family and friends. Enjoy the flayvas of *Flayvaful*.

MY STORY

I'M FROM A SMALL TOWN CALLED DERBY WHERE NOTHING REALLY HAPPENS. Picture those cowboy films where tumbleweed blows across the screen. Now I'm a chef who makes videos for a living. You couldn't make this up. I'm not sure how I got here, and a lot of people, including myself, definitely didn't think I would. Anyone who knows me, knows that I'm a shy person. I don't even use my personal social media accounts. So, if someone had said to me 3 years ago, oh you're going to be creating content full time, getting millions of views, working with names you've dreamed of and OH, YOU'RE GOING TO BE A PUBLISHED AUTHOR, I would have laughed hysterically, while also being petrified.

I didn't study cooking at school, in fact I hated cooking at school. I enjoyed history and that was it, though I was extremely lucky to have a wonderful history teacher (shout out to Mrs Goldings, an absolute superstar). I found school difficult because I often didn't have the focus, and teachers would say I had potential but I just didn't listen, or that I wasn't going to amount to much if I didn't apply myself. For me, school was like torture for my brain, I was always listening, but it's extremely difficult to remain disciplined and apply yourself to subjects you have no love for. Education in that format isn't for everyone and it certainly wasn't for me. I did leave school with some good GCSEs though because, like I said, I was always listening, even if my teachers thought I wasn't!

College was a difficult time for me. I really didn't enjoy it; the change was such a shock to the system and I realised that formal education wasn't for me. While I was at college, I took up a seasonal job and worked a Christmas event. I used to work from 6pm–2am as a waiter and it was the first time that I enjoyed what I was doing. Don't get me wrong, it wasn't fancy. The food was average at best, and that's being generous, but I loved the hustle and bustle of it all. It was only seasonal, but I really enjoyed it. I did push through and finished college, then took up an apprenticeship with great pay, great prospects and I absolutely hated it. I completed it, but I knew the rail industry wasn't for me. I tried law, payroll and product specialist roles after that, and guess what? I HATED THEM TOO. I never struggled to get jobs; I just never ever liked them.

Then I had the opportunity to move to London. I had some savings and thought f*ck it, I'm going to move and I'll get a waiting job there. I got a job, but it was cleaning tables because I didn't have enough experience, yet it was the first time I didn't dread waking up for work. I didn't think about work once I left and it worked for me. Fast forward a few weeks and I got promoted, I left and moved to another place and ended up being a sales assistant at a luxury shoe store on Jermyn Street. It was alright, but pretty boring and it didn't excite me, so I left.

This was the beautiful thing about London, you could leave a job and have another one within hours. I eventually got a waiting job again and this was the job that changed the trajectory of my life.

Up until that point I had enjoyed waiting, enjoyed telling people about the food and drinks my workplace offered. I liked seeing the finished plates and I was building my confidence by talking to loads of people every day, and let's not forget about the tips. They were fantastic. At this place, I really got along with the chefs, which is rare, as front of house and kitchen staff rarely get along. I had so much respect for them. I have a great memory, so I knew all the allergies off by heart and one day they were short a chef in the kitchen. The head chef said, 'Let's just get Nathan. We'll get him some training, get him some whites and see how it goes.' I remember being in the deep-fryer section thinking, 'Wow, this feels pretty dangerous, but I love it'. **INJECT IT!** That night there were four chefs, two events and a restaurant at 65% capacity. I was in at the deep end but I was enjoying myself. I remember the moment my head chef Luciano and sous chef Darren looked at each other, then looked at me and said, **'You're meant to be in the kitchen. We aren't letting you go back to front of house, you know that, right?'**

And that's where it started. I was keen to learn and soaked up information like a sponge. Each week I was getting more shifts in the kitchen while still working front of house. At one point I was working around 60 hours, **I was tired but I was happy.** This is where I met my best friend, Arleene, who put her all into making sure I developed my skills. She constantly pushed me and would tell me how she's known chefs who have 10 years' experience and they don't have it like me (I love you, Arleene!) and that was what I needed. She nurtured me and took me under her wing. I moved to the next job with her. This is the beautiful thing about hospitality, it has its ups and downs. **The hours are long, but you meet people along the way that become family.**

Now, the next job was soul-destroying, character-building and confidence-crushing stuff. I remember interviewing to be a chef and I didn't get the role. I learned later down the line that the feedback was that I wasn't good enough to be a chef (funny how life turns out!) but there was a floor supervisor role. I took it and it's so funny because months later they asked me to be a chef in the kitchen and even offered me a salaried role! At that point, I was pretty over this place and had bagged a job elsewhere, but lockdown came and the job fell through, so I took to TikTok and started posting videos so that I could have a catalogue of recipes to show potential employers. **Well, the videos took off**, and around 8 months after posting my first one, I was able to quit my job. Now I recipe develop, test, film and edit all my videos. It's all me and it always has been, but I guess that's my story?

BUILDING CONFIDENCE

HONESTLY, HOME COOKING IS WHERE I LEARNED 70% OF WHAT I KNOW. **Being the eldest sibling, I learned to cook from a very young age and my Jamaican heritage enabled me to see food in a different way and make the best out of very little. Jamaican food is so rich in flayvas and there's a reason why it's enjoyed round the globe. This never used to be the case though. Jamaicans were forced to make the best out of very little due to slavery. An example of this is oxtail, which was considered a scrap cut of meat way before my time. Cheap and undesirable cuts of meat were given to the enslaved and they somehow, despite the terrible conditions they faced, made the most beautiful food out of nothing. It's embedded in my DNA to be able to make something out of nothing, you know? Fast forward to adulthood, I finally gained the confidence to experiment with flavours that I love. For me, my culture is what drives my passion for cooking, along with being able to inspire people to get in the kitchen. I like to really play with traditional recipes and elevate them by adding my own twist on those original flayvas, and that's what I want you to do too.**

For me, cooking has always been my escape. It's my art and, if I'm honest, it's the only thing I'm truly good at and which comes naturally to me. Cooking is personal to the individual, it's expressive and can have different meanings for everyone. **Food makes me happy, it's my love language,** it's my way of showing love and how I like to be loved. A lot of people overcomplicate food with a bunch of crazy seasonings and, listen, this is coming from someone who grew up in a Jamaican household, not every meal or piece of meat requires ten different seasonings; sometimes the basics are all you need. Food has evolved massively; the techniques that our grandparents used to use may not be the best because food has developed since, and that's something people find hard to accept! I always say that no two Jamaican people make curried chicken the same; we all have our own little touches and that's what makes food so great. Some people find cooking daunting because, let's be honest, without trial and error it can be quite difficult to understand which flavour profiles go together and suit each other, and nobody likes putting the effort into grabbing ingredients, then working away making the food, only for it to be underwhelming and not live up to expectations. Well, guess what? We're living in a time where food is as accessible as it's ever been, where wonderful people like me go through all the trial and error so that you don't have to... **you're welcome.**

People think that you need the fanciest equipment and most expensive ingredients to create the best food but that's rubbish. I've stayed in apartments with one scratched non-stick pan that's seen better days and still managed to make the most beautiful pan-seared chicken breast, and that's because I have the knowledge. **The most important and useful thing you can have is knowledge,** which will ultimately give you confidence. There's no point having the best equipment and not knowing what temperature chicken should be cooked to...

My style of cooking is a reflection of me, my upbringing, plus a little finesse from cheffing it up in London before I started creating online content. What I'm basically saying is that I didn't go to culinary school or study anything food related. Of course, there's the cheffy way to make food and there's certain techniques that are absolute, but you're at home, not in a Michelin-star kitchen. It doesn't matter how you get your end result if I'm honest. **As long as it tastes banging, what happens from point A to point B doesn't really matter too much, does it?**

The tricky part of cooking is that it takes confidence and that's what we're going to build in this book. Now, I never used to take risks and put spins on dishes. I gained the confidence to do that from trial and error. With this book, we remove the error part. The error part is the worst part because imagine putting so much effort into trying to get a recipe right, buying the ingredients, prepping it and still getting it wrong? It's a pain. Well, don't worry about that, because, like I've said, **I've made the mistakes so you don't have to.**

THE BASICS

This section simply does what it says on the tin — it covers the basics of cooking. From ingredients to equipment and techniques, I cover the basic knowledge you'll need to understand what I'm banging on about in these recipes.

SERVINGS

Now, these are really so individual to the person. I've given rough servings because, let's be honest, some days you can eat more, some days you want to eat less. There's recipes I could eat in one sitting alone, though it's not socially acceptable, haha!

PREFERENCE

This is to do with taste and the measurements of salt. We all have different diets and none of us are built the same, so if you think there's a recipe that has too much salt, simply use less. You can always add more salt later. As you're cooking, learn to adjust the taste. If you find that something is sour, then you need to add a fat or salt. If something is too sweet, it needs an acid like lime or lemon. If something is bitter, it most likely needs to be balanced out by adding something sweet like honey or a fat like olive oil. If something is too salty, it's easy to add water to mellow it out, along with a fat and acid to cut through the flavvas.

MISE EN PLACE

This is the fancy way of saying have all your ingredients prepped and ready before you start cooking. You don't want to add oil to a pan when you haven't even minced your garlic yet. Prep is the best way to smooth cooking. So when you're looking at and reading these recipes, make sure that when it comes to getting practical you have your ingredients ready and measured.

INGREDIENTS

SALT
Unless I state otherwise, all recipes use fine salt. Please, for the love of God, don't use table salt for these recipes. I say this because the grains of table salt are so fine that 1 teaspoon of table salt vs 1 teaspoon of flaky salt will give very, very different outcomes. I always recommend using fine salt but not table salt. You can also use a coarse flaky salt or use a grinder to add salt to your recipes, that way you really control the consistency of the salt.

SEASONING
In this book I often use all-purpose seasoning, it's very common in Jamaican cooking and I use it pretty much every day. You don't have to use all-purpose seasoning as it's traditionally just a blend of dry seasonings like mixed herbs, thyme, garlic and onion etc. We thankfully live in a time where these sorts of ingredients are now readily available in most major supermarkets as well as Caribbean stores.

CURRY POWDER
In my recipes I always use Jamaican or Trinidadian curry powder. Those are my personal preferences as they are really rich in flavour and provide a wonderful colour. In the photo opposite, you'll see three types of Jamaican curry powder (clockwise from top): Betapac, Chief, and Mr Brown's.

PIMENTO BERRIES
Now, these are also called allspice. Pimento and allspice are exactly the same. Pimento berries are the whole seeds, which are stocked in Caribbean and international food stores. You'll be able to find ground pimento (allspice) in the seasoning section of most supermarkets. See photo opposite for whole pimento berries.

STOCK
When a recipe calls for stock, I like to use a stock with minimal salt. I always use stock in liquid form. Make sure you're not just banging a whole stock pot into these recipes without diluting them according to the packet instructions. For example, if a recipe calls for 150 ml (5 fl oz) of stock, don't just mix a stock pot with 150 ml (5 fl oz) of water, you'll usually need at least 400 ml (14 fl oz) of water to dilute these. If you can't get hold of a stock with minimal salt, I recommend diluting your stock or using water in these recipes instead.

BUTTERMILK
I use buttermilk quite a bit, especially for fried chicken recipes. Most supermarkets stock this; you'll find it in the dairy aisle next to the creams.

BUTTER
Unless I state otherwise, I'm always using unsalted butter, the hard stuff. You can use dairy-free or plant-based alternatives if you wish.

YEAST
I always use active dry yeast or instant yeast. Active dry yeast needs to be activated in water and instant yeast is instant... You can add instant yeast straight into your flour. Always check the packet instructions.

SCOTCH BONNET
You see this pepper on page 9? It's got a kick to it but it provides a really nice and peppery taste when added to dishes. There isn't really a pepper out there that has the same qualities for me, although habanero is the most similar. I recommend using your favourite chilli if you can't get hold of Scotch bonnet. I'm fortunate enough to live in London, so all major supermarkets stock these now.

COCONUT MILK
When I reference coconut milk, I'm referring to the tinned stuff. You need to make sure you're using coconut milk which is good quality because some coconut milks can have as little as 20% coconut, which is shocking. So always check the back of the tin.

PLANTAIN
Is it a banana? No, it's not. See the photo opposite. It looks like one and it's from the same family, but it's a lot starchier. If you fry a banana, you will not get fried plantain. You can try, but you'll be very disappointed. You can get plantain from most South East Asian and Caribbean stores. I like to shop around because the price of plantain sometimes gives me heart palpitations. In most of my recipes, especially the Plantain Breakfast Delight (see page 38), I use ripe plantain, which is the yellow one with a few dark spots (fifth down, opposite). If you're making something sweet like the Plantain Waffles on page 26, you want plantain that is very ripe. So more dark spots than yellow! If I'm personally making plantain crisps, then I'm using green plantain. This is just plantain before it's ripe and yellow.

FRESH VS DRIED INGREDIENTS
Unless I specify fresh, then just use dried ingredients. This includes herbs.

EGGS
Unless stated, please use medium free-range eggs.

OIL
Unless I specify, when I refer to oil in the recipe I'm referring to vegetable oil or any neutral oil with a high smoke point. When I say neutral, this means that the oil has little to no flavour, unlike olive oils, which are rich in flavour.

COOKING TECHNIQUES

BOIL

Boil your water, people! The mistake I see so many people make is not boiling the water properly. You'll know water is boiling because you'll see bubbles bubbling to the surface along with lots of steam. If you don't see that, your water isn't boiling. Got it?

SIMMER

Simmering is a cooking technique that involves cooking food in a liquid at a gentle, constant temperature. This method is often used for making stews, soups and sauces, and is ideal for cooking tougher cuts of meat and vegetables.

DEEP-FRYING

Now, for some reason, deep-frying seems very, very daunting to most home cooks and I get it. Hot oil is extremely dangerous and can result in some nasty injuries if it's not used correctly. However, there's so many ways to safely fry. A lot of people avoid deep-frying altogether because it might spit and pop. Well, one solution to that is a splatter screen – they are inexpensive and save you carelessly chucking ingredients in the oil and running away. If you don't have a deep-fat fryer, you can still fry. You want to make sure that you use a deep pot, because when you place anything in oil, it will start to bubble, but it only becomes unsafe if it bubbles over and onto your heat source. A heavy-bottomed pot or Dutch oven are both great alternatives. You can also buy pot-friendly baskets, which save you having to dig around in the oil to pull things out.

VISUAL CUES

You can tell if the oil is hot enough by observing it. When the oil is hot, it will start to shimmer or ripple in the pan. This is due to the heat causing the oil to expand and become less viscous.

SOUND

Another way to tell if oil is hot is by listening to it. When oil is heated to the right temperature, it will make a sizzling sound when food is added to it. If the oil is not hot enough, the food will absorb the oil and become soggy.

BREAD TEST

A quick test to determine if the oil is hot is to take a small piece of bread and drop it into the oil. If the bread immediately starts to sizzle and turn golden brown, the oil is hot enough for frying and is probably around 175–180°C (345–350°F). If you place the bread in and it sizzles quietly, then you're around the 160°C (325°F) mark. If it sizzles very quietly and gently, you're at 140–145°C (285–295°F).

It's important to note that the temperature of the oil is crucial for successful frying. If the oil is too hot, the food will burn, and if it's not hot enough, the food will be greasy and undercooked. So, while you can use visual cues, unless you're a professional, you simply won't know and it will always be a rough guess, so I really advise using a temperature probe (see page 20).

HEAT RANGES FROM DIFFERENT SOURCES

Now, some heat sources will be stronger than others. In a home kitchen, gas will provide the strongest heat source of them all. So when you're following a recipe and wondering why it says low–medium heat, it's because I'm factoring in that what's a low heat on your hob could actually be medium heat on someone else's. The same applies to oven temperatures. So really watch the temperature and rate at which your dishes are cooking.

PREHEATING

It's so, so, so important to preheat your oven and pans, so when a recipe says do it, do it!

EQUIPMENT

When it comes to cooking, these are just a few pieces that I use in my kitchen and really couldn't live without. It makes a difference in your cooking, and some of these things can take your food from good to out of this world. And that's what we're aiming for, right?

TEMPERATURE PROBE
An absolute kitchen must-have. If you have a temperature probe, you remove the guesswork. If you really want banging food with restaurant-quality flavvas at home, then you need a probe. It's a small investment but in the grand scheme of things it's absolutely worth it if you want perfect food each time. I'm sure many people are guilty of overcooking food because they would rather be safe and overcook it than guess that it's cooked. A probe solves that issue, you don't need to hack into your chicken while it's cooking and see if it's pink, just probe it!

BLENDER
If you want to be able to make seasonings like green seasoning or jerk marinade, you're going to need a blender or at least a stick blender.

SIEVE
Pretty much everyone has one. If you don't? Get one, please. Thank you!

PANS
A good cast-iron pan and one good non-stick pan is what I suggest but work with what you've got. A lot of people give non-stick pans a lot of stick – pardon the pun! But I think non-stick pans are great for building your confidence.

MIXER
It took me years to invest in a stand mixer and now that I have I haven't looked back. However, they are a pricey investment, so you can always mix by hand or use a hand-held electric mixer. Just be prepared to put in the arm work!

KITCHEN SCALES
Again, these recipes require accuracy, so I really urge you to invest in kitchen scales, especially when it comes to the Sweet Tings chapter. Desserts have little room for error and the same applies to the flatbread recipes in this book (see pages 124 and 158). If you don't weigh out your items, you simply won't get the same result.

MEASURING JUG
Again, we're all about accuracy. It's a small investment but totally worth it.

MEAT CLEANING

Now, I thought I would answer the age old question here and get it out of the way. To wash your meat or not to wash your meat? Now, I personally don't care what you do because it's honestly up to you as you're the one consuming the food.

Washing meat is often ridiculed or deemed dangerous. It's true, it can be extremely dangerous if you don't have good practices in place. When it comes to cooking professionally, it's all about removing risks. There are no risks from cooking chicken straight out of the packet because germs are killed at certain temperatures, yet there are risks of bacteria spreading from people washing chicken carelessly and incorrectly disinfecting the area.

What do I do? Well, I clean my meat, I trim excess fat away, burn away hairs, scrape the little bits of uneven skin. Depending on what meat it is, I may rub it down with salt, lime and a little water. I had the pleasure of briefly working two shifts in a chicken factory some years ago and I only managed to stomach two shifts because given the things I saw, I'm surprised I still eat meat now... haha! When it comes to getting a sear though, you need to remove all moisture from the surface of the meat, so for something like a steak, I won't clean it. Saying that, steak is usually a cleaner cut of meat. I watch my butcher slice my steaks from a whole joint that's trimmed, therefore the surface has already been prepared for me. It also falls down to how much you trust your butcher, but sometimes you don't have the time to get to your favourite butcher, so you have to go elsewhere.

Cleaning meat is something that stems from slavery – our ancestors did this as they were often given the poorest quality cuts of meat that were out of date, hence why salt and vinegar are in the equation. They were used to getting rid of the raw and 'off' smell. So, to conclude, it's a cultural thing. I won't tell you to do it and I won't tell you not to do it, so it won't be included in the recipes as it's down to personal preference. Whatever you do, make sure you're safe and comfortable.

RISE
&
SHIN

Now, I'll be honest, I'm not really a breakfast person, but over the years I've learned the hard way that people are always right when they say the best way to start your day is with a good, solid breakfast.

I've included a variety of recipes in this chapter, some are my weekly go-tos, some include hints of my Jamaican heritage and others are my every-now-and-then treat. There's honestly something for everyone and one thing I'll say is that you don't need to have crazy skills to whip up any of these dishes. However, when you do, just know that everyone is going to think you're the baddest chef in the kitchen!

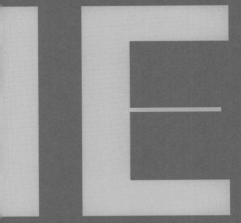

BANANA COCONUT MUFFINS

MAKES 10

200 g (7 oz) plain (all-purpose) flour
¼ teaspoon salt
1 teaspoon ground cinnamon
1 teaspoon freshly grated nutmeg
1 teaspoon baking powder
1 teaspoon bicarbonate of soda
  (baking soda)
3 ripe bananas
90 g (3¼ oz) butter or coconut oil,
  melted, plus extra (optional)
  for greasing
140 g (5 oz) light soft brown sugar
1 large egg, at room temperature
1 teaspoon vanilla bean paste
5 tablespoons coconut milk
50 g (1¾ oz) desiccated (dried
  shredded) coconut
100 g (3½ oz) icing (confectioners')
  sugar

NOW LOOK, BANANA BREAD IS NICE AND ALL — in fact, there's a recipe for that in this book — but sometimes I crave something a little smaller and quicker, so I usually whip up these babies on a weekend to have when I feel like nibbling something sweet with a coffee during the week. They're also a great treat to make with little ones.

1   Preheat the oven to 220°C fan (450°F/Gas mark 8) and spray or grease a 10-hole muffin tray with oil or fill with muffin liners.

2   In a bowl, combine the flour, salt, cinnamon, nutmeg, baking powder and bicarbonate of soda. Mix and pop to the side. In a separate bowl, mash the bananas – you could use a stand mixer or hand mixer for this part. Once mushy, beat in the melted butter, brown sugar, egg, vanilla and 3 tablespoons of the coconut milk. You want to mix this until the ingredients are just combined.

3   Once combined, gradually fold in the flour mixture using a spatula. Then add the desiccated coconut and mix until just incorporated; don't overmix – a few lumps is normal.

4   Evenly divide your batter between the holes in the tray or liners and bake in the centre of your oven for 5 minutes. Drop the temperature to 170°C fan (375°F/Gas mark 5) and bake for another 18–20 minutes. Test with a toothpick at the 22-minute mark – if there's wet batter, continue to bake for another 5 minutes; your toothpick should never be dry – a few crumbs is the sign of a perfectly cooked muffin, as it continues to cook once it leaves the oven. Allow to cool for 15 minutes before removing from the tray.

5   While the muffins cool, sift the icing sugar and combine it with the remaining 2 tablespoons of coconut milk. Drizzle over the muffins and serve.

PLANTAIN WAFFLES

MAKES 6

150 g (5½ oz) plain (all-purpose) flour
1 tablespoon baking powder
1 teaspoon ground cinnamon
½ teaspoon freshly grated nutmeg
½ teaspoon salt
100 g (3½ oz) oven-baked or steamed sweet potato, cooled
1 ripe plantain (approx. 200 g/7 oz)
60 g (2¼ oz) light soft brown sugar
1 teaspoon vanilla bean paste or extract
60 ml (4 tablespoons) vegetable oil, plus extra for coating
2 eggs, separated
200–220 ml (7–7½ fl oz) oat or cow's milk

To serve
blueberries and/or raspberries
1 banana, sliced
almond butter
golden syrup

So you've probably had waffles before or heard of them, but plantain and sweet potato waffles? Game changer, let me tell ya!

As you guys know, I love Caribbean food and where possible if I can add a likkle island flair to a dish, I'll do it! To be completely transparent, this recipe was a happy accident. When I first made these waffles, I only had one miserable plantain lying around, so I had to make it work with sweet potato and I realised it adds the perfect colour and extra layer of sweetness. The thing I love most about these waffles is that they're a great base for fried chicken, brunch or dessert. This recipe is an example of how you can add a twist to a well-loved classic. Alright, let's get into it.

1   Preheat your waffle maker to a medium–high heat.

2   Combine the flour, baking powder, cinnamon, nutmeg and salt in a bowl and pop to the side.

3   Now you want to blend together the sweet potato and plantain. Don't worry if you don't have a blender, as you can mash it instead. The little lumps of plantain provide a great texture to the waffles, plus it also means one less dish to wash! Add to the bowl.

4   Next, add the brown sugar, vanilla, vegetable oil, egg yolks and milk to the bowl. Whisk until smooth.

5   Beat the egg whites until stiff peaks form – this will take about 3–4 minutes by hand or 1 minute with an electric whisk. Carefully fold the egg whites into the batter, as you don't want to knock all the air out.

6   Spray your waffle maker with cooking spray, or brush with oil. This step is crucial, otherwise your waffles will stick.

7   Place the batter into the waffle maker, leaving about 1 cm (½ inch) gap at the edge as it will spread once you close the lid. Cook for 4–6 minutes.

8   Serve with berries, banana, almond butter and golden syrup, or place into an oven at 90°C fan (225°F/Gas mark ¼) for up to 30 minutes to keep warm until you're ready to serve.

CORNMEAL PORRIDGE

750 ml (26 fl oz) water
500 ml (17 fl oz) coconut milk
125 g (4½ oz) fine cornmeal
  (polenta)
250 g (9 oz) condensed milk
1 teaspoon freshly grated nutmeg
1 teaspoon ground cinnamon
1 teaspoon vanilla bean paste
½ teaspoon salt

You probably walk past cornmeal all the time when you're in the supermarket. You may also know it as polenta. What I do know is that this beautiful ground corn makes the best porridge. Recipes like this are staples in Jamaica and it's the stuff my grandparents grew up on. It is inexpensive and it could stretch to feed a family of ten. When I think of this porridge, it brings me sweet memories from my childhood. I vividly remember my nana giving me this on a Sunday morning as a treat sometimes and let me tell you the sweet, smooth, creamy flavvas of this porridge will have you wondering how a porridge can taste this good! The great thing is this porridge can easily be made vegan with vegan condensed milk.

1   Alright, so the first thing you want to do is place 500 ml (17 fl oz) of the water in a pot with the coconut milk and bring to a gentle boil.

2   Now, in a separate bowl, mix together the cornmeal and remaining 250 ml (9 fl oz) of water. Mix until a paste has formed, so roughly 10 seconds, and then gradually add this to your pot of boiling coconut milk and water. I find this reduces the chance of lumps forming because nobody wants a lumpy cornmeal porridge!

3   Then drop the heat to low, cover and simmer for 15 minutes, stirring every 5 minutes.

4   After 15 minutes of cooking it should have thickened and be smelling delightful! Add the condensed milk, nutmeg, cinnamon, vanilla and salt (it brings out the sweetness!).

5   Simmer for 5 more minutes over low heat and serve.

HASH BROWNS

4–5 Maris Piper potatoes (approx. 600 g/1 lb 5 oz)
vegetable oil, for frying
4 teaspoons grated onion
2½ tablespoons cornflour (cornstarch)
salt and pepper

THIS ONE'S A LOCKDOWN BABY. I think I tried to perfect all my favourite takeaway items for fun when lockdown arrived because suddenly I, like most of the country, had time and lots of it. This took a lot of testing, lots of methods and A LOT of failing, but I'm finally ready to share the perfected version of these banging, crispy, fluffy hash browns! The great thing about this recipe is that you can make the hash browns ahead of time, so I love to make a big batch once a month by tripling the recipe and freezing them once they're formed into patties. **This means I have them on hand at any given point during the month.**

1   First, peel and shred your potatoes using a grater, then add them to a bowl with ice-cold water. Move them around and agitate them to remove the starch. Cloudy water is a sign of the starch being removed. Repeat the process a few times. Drain away the excess water and strain again using a clean muslin cloth or tea towel, or as a last resort, press through a fine-mesh sieve.

2   Now, over low–medium heat, add 3 tablespoons of vegetable oil to a non-stick pan, then add the grated potato, bang in the grated onion and add a pinch of salt. Cook over low–medium heat for 20 minutes, or until the grated potato is cooked, but not mushy! It should still hold its shape and have a bite to it if you taste it.

3   Transfer the potato mixture to a bowl and sprinkle over the cornflour, 1 teaspoon of salt and a little pepper. Allow to cool for 5–10 minutes, or until it's cold enough for you to handle.

4   Form into patties by pressing the potato into moulds or moulding the potato mixture with your hands and placing the patties on a parchment-lined baking sheet. Slightly press with another tray to create flat tops. Use your fingers to reshape the sides if needed. Freeze for 45 minutes–1 hour, or until the patties are semi-frozen and stiff but not rock solid. If you're making a large batch, you'll want to place your hash browns into a Ziplock bag once they're stiff. Then keep them frozen until ready to use. They will last for 2 months in the freezer.

5   Shallow-fry in 1 cm (½ inch) of vegetable oil or deep-fry the hash browns over medium–high heat (170°C/340°F), turning every 45 seconds to get evenly golden hash browns. This should take about 2 minutes of cooking per side.

6   Place onto a wire rack to drain any excess oil, sprinkle with flaky salt and enjoy!

BREAKFAST BURRITOS

SERVES 2—4

4–6 hash browns (see page 29 for homemade)
1 green bell pepper (capsicum)
1 onion
1 jalapeño chilli (optional)
6 eggs
8 slices of smoked streaky bacon
3–4 tablespoons water
1–2 teaspoons oil
4 teaspoons butter
2–4 large tortilla wraps
sprinkle of grated spicy or smoked Cheddar
½ large avocado, sliced
hot sauce (optional)
4 tablespoons store-bought salsa verde (optional)
salt and pepper

I got HOOKED on breakfast burritos after a trip to LA, so I figured out how to satisfy my cravings. The flavvas just make so much sense to me. This one here is my go-to when I'm feeling for something a little bit naughty. You could add beans, cheese, sausages, mushrooms, chorizo. It's so simple and the ingredients are interchangeable, so the possibilities are endless!

The key to the best breakfast burritos is the layering; it has to make sense otherwise you could end up with a mushy mess when you build it. I'm no doctor but this burrito cures hangovers!

1 There's a recipe for hash browns in this book (see page 29), but if you're using frozen hash browns, then cook them according to the packet instructions.

2 Slice the pepper, onion and jalapeño. I like to keep them bite-sized or in large strips. Crack the eggs into a separate bowl and beat with a fork until the yolks and whites have mixed.

3 Next, add the bacon to a cold non-stick pan, along with the water, or enough to just cover the base of the pan, then gradually increase the heat to medium–high. This will render out the fat and give you crispy bacon! Once your bacon starts to sizzle and the water has evaporated, drizzle with the oil, turn the bacon over and cook until golden and crispy. Place on kitchen paper to soak up excess grease.

4 Then, if there's any large specks of bacon residue, remove them using kitchen paper – be sure to save some bacon grease in the pan though! Over medium heat, add the pepper, onion and chilli. Cook for 1–2 minutes, or until the onion is translucent, and pop to the side.

5 If you're using homemade hash browns, fry them now (see page 29) and leave on a wire rack to stay crispy.

6 Now add the butter to the pan; if it makes a loud sizzle, your pan is too hot, so drop the heat and remove your pan from the heat so it can cool. Stir in the eggs and cook over medium heat. Stir vigorously for 20 or so seconds. Once the eggs start to cook, remove from the heat and stir for another 20 seconds or so. Bang them back on the heat and stir every now and then. Once they start to clump together, season them with salt and pepper. Remove from the heat just before they reach your desired consistency as they will continue to cook in the residual heat of the pan.

7 Lay a tortilla wrap down, place your fillings on the lower third of the wrap, starting with the hash browns (slightly crushed), then the eggs, bacon (chopped into bite-sized pieces), grated cheese, pepper and onion, and avocado. I also like to add a little bit of hot sauce too. Fold the sides inwards over the filling and roll forward from the bottom. Tuck and roll as you go until your burrito is completely folded. Then toast in a pan over medium heat, seam-side down, for a couple of minutes and you're done! Repeat with the remaining tortillas and fillings. It's optional, but I like to serve mine with salsa verde as it's the perfect sauce for dunking and drizzling over a breakfast burrito.

VEGAN LOADED FRITTERS

SERVES 4

Fritters
400 g (14 oz) tinned young jackfruit
3 teaspoons salt
1 tablespoon olive oil
300 g (10½ oz) plain (all-purpose)
  flour
2 tablespoons roughly blitzed
  nori sheets
½ tablespoon baking powder
2 teaspoons all-purpose seasoning
2 teaspoons sugar
1 teaspoon black pepper
½ teaspoon smoked paprika
⅓ red bell pepper (capsicum),
  medium diced
⅓ green bell pepper (capsicum),
  medium diced
⅓ yellow bell pepper (capsicum),
  medium diced
1 small onion, diced
1 spring onion (scallion), diced
½ Scotch bonnet pepper (with or
  without seeds)
2 teaspoons fresh thyme leaves
200–230 ml (7–7¾ fl oz) cold water
vegetable oil, for frying

Ackee
540 g (1 lb 3 oz) tinned ackee
1 tablespoon vegetable oil
1 onion, diced
½ red bell pepper (capsicum),
  medium diced
½ green bell pepper (capsicum),
  medium diced
½ yellow bell pepper (capsicum),
  medium diced
2 garlic cloves, minced
3 sprigs of thyme, leaves picked
¼ Scotch bonnet pepper
1 spring onion (scallion), sliced,
  plus extra to garnish
1 teaspoon black pepper
½ teaspoon ground allspice
10 cherry tomatoes, whole or halved
salt
Hot Honey (page 114), for drizzling
  (or maple syrup to make it vegan)

NOW, FRITTERS ARE AN ABSOLUTE STAPLE IN CARIBBEAN CULTURE. They're typically made with salted cod, but I found a way to make my family recipe vegan without compromising on texture or flavvas! A lot of people are sometimes scared to veganise recipes as they're not sure how to or don't want something that doesn't really live up to the original dish. As someone who eats meat, I can tell you now, these are BANGING! In this recipe it's the little things that make a huge difference. The addition of nori sheets and jackfruit really takes these fritters to the next level. The amount of salt may seem excessive but what we're doing is essentially replicating what's traditionally done with salted cod.

I don't like to do traditional things the traditional way, as you'll learn from this wonderful book. This is a recipe which showcases that. This one isn't too crazy — think of it as me easing you into my creations. I really, really love ackee. It's vegan but honestly loved by the majority of Jamaican people. It's creamy, kinda nutty, kinda buttery and completely unique in taste. Fun fact, ackee is a fruit and when it's unripe it's poisonous, but don't worry — it's pretty hard to get hold of unripe ackee if you don't have the pleasure of living in the Caribbean, so you won't be likely to die any time soon! Ackee is incredibly fragile, so it's really important that you handle the ackee like a newborn baby. Treat it with caution. Ya hear?

1   The first thing you want to do is drain the water from your jackfruit, then bang it in a bowl and break it into smaller pieces either using your hands or a fork. Then season with the salt. Cover and let this sit for 30 minutes: this is going to draw out the moisture, which will prevent the jackfruit from tasting mushy. It's also going to season it and I find this is the best method to replicate that 'salted cod' taste.

2   Place the jackfruit in a muslin cloth or clean tea towel and squeeze out the excess moisture. Then, in a pan over a medium heat, add the oil, then the jackfruit and sauté for 5 minutes. The purpose of this is to cook the jackfruit and dry it out.

3   While your jackfruit is cooling, combine the flour, nori, baking powder, all-purpose seasoning, sugar, black pepper and smoked paprika. Whisk together, then add half the bell peppers, onion, spring onion and the cooked but cooled jackfruit. Give it a mix and pop to the side.

4   I like to blend the remaining peppers, onion and spring onion along with the Scotch bonnet and thyme, as I personally think this creates the perfect texture – I don't like big old chunks of pepper

continued overleaf

bombarding every bite! Add your blended pepper mixture to the jackfruit mixture and gradually mix in half your water. Once it starts to come together, you want to continue to add the remaining water. It should resemble a thick porridge-like consistency that will still pour from a spoon.

5   Cover and allow to sit for 30 minutes; this allows the flour to really soak up the ingredients, which yields better fritters.

6   Now, in a non-stick pan, you want to add enough oil to shallow-fry these, so roughly 5 mm–1 cm (¼–½ inch) deep. Heat the oil over medium–high heat and, once your oil is hot, drop down to medium heat. (Test with a toothpick or wooden spoon. If the spoon or toothpick bubbles when you place it in, your oil is hot enough.) Dollop the fritter mixture into the pan, just like for pancakes (so around 7.5 cm/3 inches wide). The bigger they are, the longer they'll take to cook through. You want to cook these for 2–3ish minutes per side. The edges should be crispy, yet golden. Place on kitchen paper to soak up any excess grease as you fry the remaining fritters.

7   For the ackee, you want to pour it into a sieve to drain it. Leave suspended over a bowl or pot to catch any remaining juices.

8   In a non-stick pan over medium heat, add the oil, onion, bell peppers and garlic. Cook for 2–3 minutes, or until the peppers and onion have started to soften. Now you want to add in the thyme leaves along with the Scotch bonnet, spring onion, black pepper, allspice and tomatoes. Stir and cook for another 2–3 minutes, or until the tomatoes have started to blister/burst and break down.

9   Finally, carefully add the ackee to the pan, DO NOT STIR IT! You want to lift and fold with a spatula to get the ingredients incorporated. Cook for a minute or two, taste and sprinkle with a little salt.

10   Stack your fritters up, then serve your ackee on top with a garnish of spring onions and hot honey.

TROPICAL BREAKFAST FRUIT BARS

MAKES 14–16

180 g (6 oz) whole oats
100 g (3½ oz) light soft brown sugar
1½ teaspoons baking powder
1 teaspoon ground cinnamon
½ teaspoon salt
2 large eggs
200 ml (7 fl oz) oat milk
2 tablespoons coconut oil
1 teaspoon vanilla bean paste
  or extract
4 tablespoons apple sauce
3 tablespoons coconut flakes
3 tablespoons dried pineapple
  chunks
5 tablespoons chopped almonds

THESE ARE LITTLE SNACKS I MAKE FOR THE WEEK. **I usually have them when I need an energy boost or want something to nibble on after breakfast. They're really good to have on the go in the mornings too, especially if you're feeling for something light. You'll probably wonder why apple sauce is listed in the ingredients, but it's absolutely key to keeping these moist and it adds a bit of fruitiness and sweetness. One of these bars and a large banana and I'm ready to start my day! I absolutely loved baking with my nana when I was little, so every time I make these bars, I wake up my inner child, and naturally these are a really good introductory snack to bake with the little ones.**

1   Preheat the oven to 170°C (375°F/Gas mark 5) and line a 23 cm (9 inch) square tin with baking parchment.

2   The first thing you want to do is combine your dry ingredients. Bang the oats, sugar, baking powder, cinnamon and salt in a bowl and mix with a whisk. I like to use a whisk as it breaks down any sugar clumps.

3   In a separate bowl, combine the eggs, oat milk, coconut oil, vanilla and apple sauce. Whisk together, then add the mixed dry ingredients along with the coconut flakes, pineapple and almonds and fold in.

4   Pour into the prepared tin and bake for 30 minutes or until nice and golden. Remove from the oven and allow to cool for at least 45 minutes.

5   Slice into even-sized pieces and store in an airtight container to retain freshness. These will keep for 3–4 days.

ULTIMATE BREAKFAST MUFFIN

MAKES 3 DOUBLE MUFFINS
OR 6 SINGLES

500 g (1 lb 2 oz) pork mince
(20% fat) or 8 pork sausages,
skin removed
8 tablespoons Scotch Bonnet Honey
Sauce (page 212)
1 tablespoon ketchup
½ teaspoon Worcestershire sauce
oil, for cooking
6 slices of American cheese
¼ onion, sliced into 6 rings
3–6 eggs
3–6 English breakfast muffins,
toasted
3–6 teaspoons red onion chutney

Pork rub (optional)
1 tablespoon light soft brown sugar
1½ teaspoons salt
1 teaspoon black pepper
1 teaspoon onion powder
1 teaspoon garlic powder
1 teaspoon smoked paprika
½ teaspoon ground cumin
½ teaspoon cayenne pepper

YOU SEE THIS BREAKFAST MUFFIN? YEAH, IT'S DIFFERENT. **If you think you've already had the best breakfast muffin from a certain fast food chain that shall not be named for legal reasons, then think again. I'm here to tell you that you simply haven't and that this breakfast muffin is THE BEST. Double-smashed seasoned pork sausage patties, cheese, my signature breakfast sauce, a perfectly runny fried egg, red onion chutney and all encompassed in a soft toasted English muffin.** It's a FLAYVA explosion that makes so much sense. **Is it a little work? Yes. Is it worth it? Abso-fuc*ing-lutely.**

There are a few tricks to making this better than any takeaway breakfast muffin and one is selecting the right ingredients. You want to use a pork mince that's 20% fat and if you can't get hold of pork mince, then your favourite sausages out of the casing will do. The freshness of the sliced onions helps intensify the meaty flavour of the pork while also cutting through the fat. The honey Scotch bonnet brekkie sauce really adds a nice little bit of heat and spice, but the subtle sweetness of the honey keeps it balanced. American cheese is a must in my opinion. Now, a lot of people would ask 'Why aren't you using better quality cheese?' Blah, blah, blahhhhhh. To me the cheese is the beauty of this breakfast muffin — you don't want a strong cheese, you want a subtle cheese that will act as the glorious glue. Lastly, that final lick of onion chutney helps cut through the richness of a runny yolk or soft scrambled eggs.

1   If using pork mince, first make the pork rub. In a bowl, combine the sugar, salt, pepper, onion powder, garlic powder, smoked paprika, cumin and cayenne pepper. Season the pork with all of the rub, portion into 6 balls and refrigerate until ready to use.

2   To make my brekkie sauce, combine the Scotch bonnet honey sauce, ketchup and Worcestershire sauce, then pop to the side.

3   Set a pan over medium–high heat, then lightly grease the pan with oil. Grab your pork balls and either use a burger press or a spatula wrapped in foil to press down and smash each one into a patty, just like a burger. Cook each patty for 1½ minutes, then flip. Top with a slice of cheese and 1 onion ring and cook for a further 1½ minutes. If you're making doubles, only the top sausage patty needs the onion slice.

4   Heat another pan over medium–high heat, add 2 tablespoons of oil and crack your eggs into an egg mould if you're feeling fancy. Alternatively, you can just crack them into the pan or soft scramble them (see page 30). Fry your eggs for 1–2 minutes, then add 2 tablespoons of water to the pan and cover with a lid – this will create steam which will cook the whites of the eggs but still leave runny yolks. Cook for a further 30 seconds–1 minute and that's your eggs done.

5   Now you just need to assemble your muffins. It goes toasted muffin half, brekkie sauce, sausage patty (or two), egg, a dollop of red onion chutney and close with the toasted muffin half spread with some more brekkie sauce.

The pork rub is a game changer, but if you're using sausages, then you can skip this step because they're already seasoned.

PLANTAIN BREAKFAST DELIGHT

SERVES 2–4

Pico de gallo
½ onion, diced
1 jalapeño chilli, diced
juice of 1 lime
1 tablespoon olive oil
1 teaspoon salt
3 large ripe but firm tomatoes
3 tablespoons fresh coriander
  (cilantro)
pinch of black pepper

Garlic mushrooms
500 g (1 lb 2 oz) button mushrooms
1 tablespoon olive oil
2–3 tablespoons salted butter
1 teaspoon fresh thyme leaves
1½ tablespoons minced garlic
½ teaspoon chilli flakes
1 spring onion (scallion), chopped

Plantain
4 medium ripe plantains
5–6 tablespoons vegetable oil
1 onion, small diced
2 garlic cloves, minced
1 teaspoon fresh thyme leaves
2 teaspoons oregano
1 teaspoon smoked paprika
1 teaspoon Cajun seasoning
1 teaspoon black pepper
2 teaspoons butter
3 tablespoons ketchup

Scrambled eggs
6 eggs
6 teaspoons butter
salt and pepper
1 tablespoon chopped fresh
  chives, to garnish (optional)

I LOVE PLANTAIN AND PLANTAIN LOVES ME, I don't know if you've noticed? My goodness, it's just so beautiful, truly a work of art. People always ask me what a plantain is — it looks like a banana, but it certainly doesn't taste like one. Think of plantain as a banana's starchier distant cousin. Its flavour profile changes depending on its ripeness but it's starchy even when ripe, so unlike a banana, when you fry it, it holds its shape. Though it's sweet, it doesn't have that banana taste. It's just unique.

The proof is in the name: this recipe is simply delightful, guys! When it comes to cooking plantain, you'll find a lot of people like to keep it simple because it's banging as it is but, trust me, turning a classic into a savoury dish with the addition of herbs and spices isn't a bad thing. This recipe is next level flayvas, I'm telling you! It's easily one of my favourite weekend breakfasts. Sweet but savoury plantain, soft scrambled eggs, avocados and pico de gallo, what's not to love? If sweet plantain isn't your thing, then you can easily use green or unripe plantain.

A lot of people will think I'm crazy, but ketchup is the secret ingredient that ties the plantain together. It's really, really common to use ketchup in Jamaican cooking because tomato paste is expensive and less readily available. I had a strong Jamaican and American influence around me growing up, so these were the little secrets I picked up along the way.

1   Alright, so the first thing you want to make is your pico de gallo. It's the easiest thing to do and it can chill in the refrigerator while you prepare everything else. In a bowl, combine the diced onion, jalapeño, lime juice, olive oil and salt. Let the flayvas marinate while you dice the tomatoes and roughly chop the coriander.

2   Then add the chopped tomatoes, coriander and black pepper. Taste and adjust the seasoning if needed. Let this sit in the refrigerator until ready to use.

3   Now, for the garlic mushrooms, slice your larger mushrooms in half, but if they're small keep 'em whole. Set a pan over medium–high heat. Once hot, add the oil and butter along with the mushrooms. Sauté for 3–5 minutes, or until the mushrooms are nice and golden.

4   Now it's time to add the flayvas! Add the fresh thyme, garlic, chilli flakes and spring onion to the mushrooms. Toss and get everything acquainted before finishing with salt and pepper.

5   For the plantain, remove the plantain skin, and I like to chop it into bite-sized cubes. Heat a large non-stick pan over medium heat along with the oil, you need around 1–2 cm (½–¾ inch) of oil. Add the plantain and cook on all sides for 5 or so minutes, or until golden.

continued overleaf

Make sure your plantain sizzles when it comes into contact with the oil, otherwise you'll be left with greasy plantain! Ensure you're turning it often as it will start to burn; if you find it's cooking too quickly, simply drop the heat.

6   Once cooked, drop the heat to low, remove any oil left in the pan and add the diced onion, garlic and thyme. Toss and allow to cook for 2 minutes. Now add your oregano, smoked paprika, Cajun seasoning, pepper, butter and ketchup. Cook for another 2–3 minutes and that's done.

7   **For the eggs, I like to keep it simple with a basic soft scrambled egg,** which takes less than 5 minutes to come together. Crack your eggs into a bowl with no shells… please. Whisk with a fork until the whites and yolks are mixed.

8   Heat a non-stick pan over low–medium heat, then add the butter. If it sizzles loudly, your pan is too hot, so ease off the heat!

9   Once the butter has melted, add the eggs and stir vigorously for 20–30 seconds. Once they start to cook, remove from the heat, then stir for another 20 seconds or so. Bang them back on the heat and stir every now and then. Once they start to clump together, season with salt and pepper. Remove from the heat just before they reach your desired consistency as they will continue to cook in the residual heat of the pan.

10 Serve everything together immediately in a bowl and garnish with some chives if you're feeling extra boujee!

JERK-SPICED MUSHROOM BREKKIE

SERVES 2

1 avocado
1 teaspoon lime juice
1 teaspoon chilli flakes
½ teaspoon salt
½ teaspoon black pepper
½ teaspoon smoked paprika
450 g (1 lb) oyster mushrooms,
   or button mushrooms
1 tablespoon olive oil
2 tablespoons butter, plus
   2 teaspoons for the mushrooms
1–2 teaspoons Dry Jerk Rub
   (page 208)
2–4 slices of sourdough
chopped fresh chives, to garnish

SIMPLE FLAYVAS DONE WELL, THAT'S WHAT THIS IS. **Nothing crazy, nothing complicated, it comes together in 15 minutes but tastes like such an amazing treat.** Recipes like this get you comfortable cooking because they're basically foolproof. **Butter makes everything taste better, but a little goes a long way, and you can even leave it out if you wish.**

Now, I'm a meat eater, but for the last few years I've tried to make a conscious effort to reduce the amount of meat I eat. Mushrooms have always been a great alternative to meat, they take on flayva so incredibly well, they're not too expensive and they are readily available pretty much everywhere. The addition of jerk seasoning just adds a little oomph, it's different but it's banging, and it doesn't take loads of steps to get right.

1   To make your smashed avocado, add the avocado to a bowl along with the lime juice, chilli flakes, salt, pepper and smoked paprika, then mash with a fork. Refrigerate until ready to use. See, I told you it's simple!

2   Grab the oyster mushrooms, brush off any debris and tear into chunks. If you're using king oyster mushrooms, slice them in half.

3   Preheat a pan over medium–high heat. Once hot, add the oil and the 2 teaspoons of butter, toss in the mushrooms and cook for 2–5 minutes until nice and golden, depending on the type of mushroom you're using. You should hear a sizzle when you add the mushrooms – that's the sign of a correctly heated pan.

4   Once cooked, season with your jerk seasoning and pop to the side.

5   Heat a pan over medium heat, add the 2 tablespoons of butter and toast your bread for 1–2 minutes, this is the key to creating flayva. The butter makes the bread perfectly golden and, like I said above, butter makes everything taste better. Remove from the pan once golden.

6   Spread the smashed avocado on your toasted sourdough, top with the mushrooms and a few freshly chopped chives!

SALTFISH FRITTERS

MAKES 12–15

450 g (1 lb) saltfish
300 g (10½ oz) plain (all-purpose)
  flour
1 tablespoon baking powder
2 teaspoons all-purpose seasoning
2 teaspoons sugar
1 teaspoon salt
1 teaspoon black pepper
½ teaspoon smoked paprika
1 bell pepper (capsicum), diced
  (I use a mix of green and red)
1 small onion, diced
½ Scotch bonnet pepper, minced
3 sprigs of fresh thyme, leaves
  picked
200–230 ml (7–7¾ fl oz) cold water
vegetable oil, for frying
Scotch Bonnet Honey Sauce
  (page 212), to serve (optional)

THESE ARE OG FRITTERS, THE BAD BOI FRITTERS, the fritters that you could demolish in one sitting, alone with absolutely no help! I'm biased and think mine are the best and I know you'll think that too.

Now, there's variations of these throughout the Caribbean, but they originate from Jamaica. Some may know them as Stamp and Go and traditionally it's something I've always had for breakfast, but they are also available throughout the day at most takeaways or served as a starter in restaurants. It doesn't matter what time of day you have them, because they taste banging regardless, ya hear me? When my nana used to make fritters in the morning, I knew it was going to be a good day, an excellent one even. It's mad because they're so simple, there's nothing crazy or complicated but it just works, and that's Jamaican food for you in one sentence, really!

Back in the day, all these ingredients were so cheap, especially the salted cod. It would be imported from the North Atlantic, and with it being salted it would survive the journey as the salt was a natural preservative. Essentially, it was a cheap way for plantation owners to feed the enslaved. Over the years, we reclaimed this, added our own flair and turned it into a staple that's enjoyed by many. It's important to never forget the origin of these dishes because there's so much rich history in Jamaican food.

1   The first thing you want to do is place your saltfish in a large pot and cover it with cold water. Then place over high heat and bring to the boil. Once boiling, drain the water, cover with fresh cold water and repeat the process. After you've boiled the fish twice, give it a taste and if it's too salty, give it another boil. The fish should still taste a little salty but it shouldn't be overbearing.

2   Once done, drain all the excess water and allow the saltfish to cool. Once cool enough to handle, break into bite-sized chunks – the saltfish will break down more once combined with other ingredients.

3   In a bowl, combine your flour, baking powder, all-purpose seasoning, sugar, salt, black pepper and smoked paprika and whisk together. Then add your saltfish and half the bell peppers and onion. Give it a mix and pop to the side.

4   I like to blend the remaining onion and pepper, along with the Scotch bonnet and thyme, as I think this creates the perfect texture for saltfish fritters because I just hate it when there's loads of chunks, but you can skip this step and keep 'em whole.

5   Add the blended onion to your mixture along with half the cold water and mix. Then gradually stir in the remaining water, this should only take 1–2 minutes and it should resemble a thick porridge-like consistency that will still pour from a spoon.

6   Cover and allow to sit for 30 minutes – this allows the flour to really soak up the ingredients.

7   Set a pan over medium heat and add enough oil so it's 1 cm (½ inch) in depth. Spoon the saltfish mixture into the pan to create 7.5 cm (3 inch) oval shapes. The shape doesn't really matter, so don't worry if they are odd sizes – it adds character! Fry for about 2 minutes per side or until nice and golden. Then place on kitchen paper to drain any excess oil.

8   To deep-fry, place around 7.5–10 cm (3–4 inches) of oil in a heavy-bottomed pot over high heat. Dip your tablespoon in the oil, then into your batter and drop the batter carefully into the oil. Repeat the process until your pot is full of balls, yet there's still room for them to cook. Allow them to cook for 2–3 minutes, turning every now and then for even cooking.

9   I like to serve mine with Scotch bonnet honey sauce.

GREEN SMOOTHIE GOODNESS

MAKES 1–2

1 large handful of spinach
1 banana
100 g (3½ oz) frozen pineapple
100 g (3½ oz) frozen mango
1 teaspoon honey
1 tablespoon flaxseed
1 teaspoon sea-moss (optional)
300 ml (10½ fl oz) coconut water

Now, I don't know about you, but there's times when I just don't want a big old breakfast or I'm feeling sluggish first thing. I don't skip breakfast, so I need something to sustain me and keep me going. I also find it hard to get in my five-a-day, but when I have this shake, I give myself a great head start. I have this a couple of times a week and it NEVER fails me. If you're into the gym, you can easily add some protein powder and oats to bulk it out too.

1   In a blender, combine all the ingredients. Blend until smooth and consume within 5 hours.

MAII
FLAY

A collection of recipes that hit every spot, from quick midweek meals to show-off flayvas to impress your loved ones. There's something for everyone here.

ONE-PAN SWEET CHILLI ROAST CHICKEN

SERVES 4–6

6 skin-on, bone-in chicken legs
600 g (1 lb 5 oz) red potatoes,
  cut into bite-sized pieces
2 red onions, quartered
8 sprigs of fresh thyme
2 carrots, peeled and roughly
  chopped into 3 cm (1¼ inch)
  chunks
olive oil, for drizzling
200 ml (7 fl oz) chicken stock
6–8 tablespoons sweet chilli sauce
salt and pepper
chopped fresh chives, to garnish
  (optional)

Chicken seasoning
2 tablespoons light soft brown sugar
1 tablespoon all-purpose seasoning
1 tablespoon dried oregano
1 teaspoon black pepper
2 teaspoons salt
2 teaspoons onion powder
1 teaspoon smoked paprika
½ teaspoon cayenne pepper
4 tablespoons olive oil
45 g (1½ oz) salted butter, melted
juice of 1 lemon
5 garlic cloves, grated

THIS MEAL HERE IS ONE OF MY FAVOURITES. Sometimes I just want to bang everything in a tray and let it do its thing in the oven while I relax. Now, just because it's easy doesn't mean that it's basic. This recipe is still very much full of flavvas and you honestly can't go wrong with skin–on oven–roasted chicken. Sweet, sticky skin–on chicken that effortlessly falls off the bone? Yeah, that's my type of comfort dinner right there.

This one here is something I like to marinate and prepare the night before; I like to think of it as a gift from present me to future me! **That way all I have to do is add the stock and bang it in the oven and it feels even easier.**

1   Combine all the chicken seasoning ingredients in a bowl. I recommend starting with 1 teaspoon of salt, then taste the marinade and adjust if needed. Then use the marinade to season the chicken legs, being sure to get under the thigh skin with the seasoning. This will ensure the flavvas penetrate the meat!

2   For best results, marinate overnight in the refrigerator, but if you don't have time, it's fine to skip this part. Just know that even an hour of marinating makes a huge difference!

3   Preheat the oven to 200°C fan (425°F/Gas mark 7).

4   Now add the potatoes to a baking dish, along with the onions, thyme and carrots. Drizzle with a little olive oil and sprinkle with salt and pepper.

5   Then add the marinated chicken to the dish, skin-side up, making sure it's nestled in with the potatoes and not sitting on top. This ensures that everything cooks at roughly the same speed.

6   We don't waste a drop of flavva, so pour the chicken stock into the bowl that you marinated the chicken in and give it a swirl. This will catch any remaining seasoning. Then add the stock directly to the pan, not on the chicken.

7   Cover with foil or an ovenproof lid (this will create steam, which will speed up the potatoes cooking and keep the chicken moist) and roast for 50 minutes.

8   Remove the foil and cook for a further 20 minutes, basting the chicken and potatoes every 10 minutes. Then add about 1 tablespoon of sweet chilli sauce on top of each chicken leg and roast for another 5–10 minutes. If you're feeling a little boujee, garnish with some freshly chopped chives!

Marinating your meat for even just an hour makes a difference, but it's honestly not the be all and end all.

PEPPERED STEAK PIE

OH BOY, IS THIS ONE SPECIAL. **The steak sizzles away, forcing the beautiful aromas of fragrant spices around the kitchen. One thing you'll always notice with Jamaican food is that a lot of our staple recipes don't break the bank and never fail to make you feel warm and cosy.**

This is another one of those dishes where I combine the best of British with Jamaican cuisine. I love a good pie, but they can sometimes just lack excitement, however, this one never falls short. I also love that it's not hard to make.

Whether you're reminiscing about your childhood or creating new memories with your family, this Jamaican peppered steak pie fusion recipe is sure to become a staple in your home. So go ahead, give it a try and indulge in the rich and beautiful Jamaican flayvas of this delicious dish.

SERVES 4–8

1 kg (2 lb 4 oz) skirt steak, sliced into 2 cm (¾ inch) thick strips (against the grain)
3 teaspoons all-purpose seasoning
1 teaspoon salt
1 teaspoon black pepper
1 teaspoon ground allspice
4 teaspoons gravy browning
2 tablespoons reduced-sodium light soy sauce
500 ml (17 fl oz) reduced-sodium beef stock
4 tablespoons ketchup
1 tablespoon Worcestershire sauce
1–2 tablespoons vegetable oil
6 garlic cloves, minced
2 teaspoons minced fresh ginger
1 Scotch bonnet pepper, deseeded and minced
1 large onion, sliced
4 spring onions (scallions), sliced
½ large red bell pepper (capsicum), sliced
½ large green bell pepper (capsicum), sliced
½ large yellow or orange bell pepper (capsicum), sliced
8 sprigs of fresh thyme, leaves picked
4 tablespoons cornflour (cornstarch)
5 tablespoons water
375 g (13 oz) sheet of ready-rolled puff pastry
1 egg yolk, mixed with 2 tablespoons water

1. In a large mixing bowl, combine the sliced skirt steak with the all-purpose seasoning, salt, pepper, allspice, 2 teaspoons of browning and the soy sauce. Mix well, cover and marinate the steak in the refrigerator for at least 2 hours, or overnight for best results.

2. To make the sauce, combine the beef stock, ketchup, remaining 2 teaspoons of browning and the Worcestershire sauce.

3. In a large pan or Dutch oven, heat 1 tablespoon of oil over medium–high heat. Brown off the steak pieces for 3–4 minutes, then add the garlic and ginger. Cook for a further minute, stirring regularly. If you find that your steak has released a lot of moisture, drain this away and reserve it for later.

4. Add the Scotch bonnet pepper, onion, spring onions, peppers and thyme and get them coated in all those flayvas! Once your onions have softened and everything is smelling fragrant, bang in the sauce and stir.

5. Cover with a lid and let the steak simmer over low–medium heat for 30 minutes. Check after 15–20 minutes to ensure the liquid is still there and bubbling away and add a few tablespoons of hot water if needed. Preheat the oven to 180°C fan (400°F/Gas mark 6).

6. Combine the cornflour and water in a small bowl, pour half the mixture into the pan and stir over low heat until it starts to thicken. If the sauce still isn't starting to get thick like a gravy after 5 minutes, then continue to add your cornflour mixture until it does. Add your reserved cooking juices, if you have any, and allow to simmer for 5 more minutes. The sauce should have thickened, and your meat should be tender but still hold its shape. If you have barely any sauce, add water or stock until a gravy forms again. Adjust the seasoning with salt and pepper if needed, but you should be good.

7. Place the meat into a pie dish and roll the pastry on top, trim and then press the edges onto the dish to seal. Re-roll the trimmings and use them to decorate the pie with shapes. Make two small slits in the centre of your pie to ensure the steam can escape. Brush the top of the pastry with the egg yolk mixture.

8. Bake for 25–30 minutes until the pastry is golden brown and crispy. Let the pie cool for a few minutes before slicing and serving. Enjoy!

CHILLI BUTTER BAKED SALMON

SERVES 6

900 g–1 kg (2 lb–2 lb 4 oz) salmon
   fillet, skin on
2–4 tablespoons olive oil
125 g (4½ oz) butter
2 tablespoons gochujang paste
   (or 3 tablespoons harissa paste)
1 tablespoon gochugaru
1 tablespoon sesame oil
1½ tablespoons minced garlic
2 teaspoons honey
salt and pepper
lime wedges, to serve

SALMON IS ONE OF MY GO–TO FISH, it tastes bloody amazing and it's so easy to cook even if you think you don't know what you're doing. Trust me, people try my salmon and they're left speechless. They're even more speechless when I tell them exactly how I did it. It's really that good. There's no crazy techniques to this one. Just an oven, some spices and a whole load of butter!

Now, over the years I've tested the optimum cooking temperature for salmon because you really do need different temperatures with different sized pieces. I prefer a more aggressive heat when cooking smaller fillets of salmon, but this is just a little too harsh for whole sides, like the one I'm using for this recipe.

Gochujang and gochugaru really take the throne here. Gochugaru is a Korean chilli flake, bright red and varying in coarseness. Gochujang is a thick Korean chilli paste that's bold in flayva, sweet, spicy and has a slight umami kick. Now, you can find gochujang in a lot of supermarket international aisles these days or online. It's not the end of the world if you can't get these ingredients, and I would suggest going down the Middle Eastern route and using a harissa paste instead as it's so easily available and will still give you that spicy kick. It's really important that you either make a foil boat for your salmon or use baking parchment so the skin doesn't stick, because honestly that's a pain you don't want to experience.

1   Allow the salmon to sit at room temperature for 15–30 minutes and preheat the oven to 180°C fan (400°F/Gas mark 6).

2   Pat the salmon dry, drizzle with the olive oil and massage this in. Then generously season with salt and pepper, just like you would season a steak. Now, if you don't know how you would season a steak, simply season your salmon from a height to ensure even coverage. About 20–25 cm (8–10 inches) above the salmon should do the trick.

3   Bake the salmon for 13–15 minutes, or until the chunkiest and thickest part reads 50–55°C (122–131°F). Allow the salmon to rest for 5–7 minutes.

4   While your salmon is resting, melt the butter with the gochujang, gochugaru, sesame oil, minced garlic and honey. Whisk over medium heat until combined – you don't want to thicken the sauce.

5   Pour your glorious chilli butter over the salmon and serve with a few wedges of lime. Tuck in and enjoy!

GUAVA LIME GLAZED BEEF SHORT RIBS

SERVES 4

6 x 400 g (14 oz) beef short ribs
1 tablespoon Dry Jerk Rub
  (page 208)
1 teaspoon ground allspice
2 teaspoons salt
1 teaspoon black pepper
3 tablespoons vegetable oil
1 large onion, small diced
4 garlic cloves, minced
2 carrots, peeled and small diced
1 rib of celery, small diced
2 tablespoons Wet Jerk Marinade
  (page 207)
1 tablespoon tomato paste
  (concentrated purée)
5 sprigs of fresh thyme
500 ml (17 fl oz) dry red wine
3 teaspoons Worcestershire sauce
600 ml (21 fl oz) beef stock
75 ml (2½ fl oz) spiced rum
5 tablespoons guava jam
zest and juice of 1 lime
chopped fresh chives, to garnish
Creamy Garlic Mash (page 103),
  to serve

BEEF SHORT RIBS ARE ABSOLUTELY, HANDS DOWN, THE BEST RIBS IN THE GAME. **With ridiculous amounts of tender, succulent fall-off-the-bone meat, what's not to love? Low and slow is the only way to go when it comes to these chunky beef short ribs. It just means that all that marbling you see through the meat has the chance to break down and, once you do that, you're in heaven.**

Over the years, beef short ribs have become widely available, and you can get them from pretty much any supermarket these days. I prefer to get mine from the butcher because that way you have absolute control on the size, meat-to-fat ratio and the quality. You guys know me, when it comes to flavvas, I don't play, and this beef short rib recipe creates a tropical yet rich meaty explosion with every bite. **These ribs are coated in a dry jerk rub, seared and slow-cooked in a rich red wine beef broth filled with vegetables that soak up all dem good herbs and aromatic spices! We then use the cooking juices at the end to create a sweet, sticky spiced rum glaze.**

Guava jam is definitely unique. It can be found in some supermarkets, but you'll definitely find it in most, if not all, Afro-Caribbean markets. If you can't get hold of it, you can use a redcurrant jelly to bring in the sweetness. If you don't drink alcohol, that's absolutely fine. This recipe still works beautifully without it — just double up on stock instead.

1   If cooking in the oven, preheat the oven to 175°C fan (385°F/Gas mark 5½).

2   Pat your short ribs down – you want to remove any unwanted moisture. This will get us a nice crust and colour when we sear them. Mix the dry jerk rub, allspice, salt and pepper together, then use it to evenly coat your ribs.

3   Heat the oil in a large pan (or ovenproof dish for oven method) over medium heat. You want to sear the top and two sides of the ribs; there's no need to sear the bottom. Be careful when searing as seasoning will burn when exposed to very high temperatures. Cook for about 2 minutes per side, or until a nice golden crust has formed. Remove the ribs and pop to the side.

4   Reduce the heat to low-medium, then add the onion, garlic, carrots and celery. Cook for 2–3 minutes, or until softened. Then go in with the wet jerk marinade, tomato paste and thyme and cook for a further 2 minutes.

5   Now deglaze the pan with the wine, Worcestershire sauce and stock. Stir well and be sure to scrape the bottom and get all those flayvas.

6   If you're using a slow cooker or pressure cooker, add all the cooking juices from the pan and then submerge the ribs. If using a slow cooker, cook on high for 4 hours or on low for 8 hours. If using a pressure cooker, cook on high for 1 hour.

7   If you're cooking in the oven, return the ribs to the liquid, arrange them so they are submerged, cover with a lid and transfer to the preheated oven for 2–2½ hours, depending on the size of the ribs.

8   If cooking on the hob, cover with baking parchment so the meat isn't exposed, then a lid, and simmer gently over low heat for 3 hours.

9   Once done, your ribs should easily pull apart with a fork. Cover the ribs so they remain moist while you make your sauce. Strain the cooking juices and press all of those juices and goodness out using a sieve – you want about 500 ml (17 fl oz). Once you have this rich liquid gold, add the spiced rum and simmer over medium heat, or until thickened.

10   Once thickened, add the guava jam, lime zest and juice. At this point you can adjust the seasoning if needed. **Now, to get the ribs nice and sticky, carefully add them back into the sauce and baste for a few minutes over medium heat.** Serve on a bed of creamy garlic mash and with a generous sprinkling of fresh chives.

LEMON SALMON PASTA

SERVES 2–4

500 g (1 lb 2 oz) spaghetti
2 x 150 g (5½ oz) salmon fillets
2 teaspoons vegetable oil
1–2 teaspoons Lemon Pepper
  Seasoning (page 201)
½ teaspoon chilli flakes
2 teaspoons butter
1 shallot, diced, or ½ onion, diced
4 garlic cloves, minced
½ teaspoon fresh thyme leaves
250 ml (9 fl oz) double (heavy)
  cream
½ teaspoon fresh lemon juice
zest of ½ lemon
1 tablespoon roughly chopped dill,
  plus extra to serve
¾ teaspoon salt
1 teaspoon black pepper

THIS IS MY GO-TO PASTA RECIPE. **Now, if you haven't noticed, I'm not really a pasta person... don't shoot me, I know it's weird. Don't get me wrong, I love a good old lasagne or bolognese, but I never order pasta when I go out. It's only recently that I've really started cooking pasta at home. I grew up on rice as my go-to, but this recipe here? I love it.** It's what I whip up midweek when I need something quick, yet tasty. **I can also get bored of rice, so this is a great alternative.**

Salmon and dill are such a beautiful pairing, the sauce is creamy, garlicky, kinda herby and it's just a beautifully balanced dish. I use my lemon pepper seasoning in this recipe as less is more when it comes to the salmon for this one. I love that in this recipe the salmon goes a long way because pasta is naturally so filling. Saying that, I could easily smash this all down by myself... DON'T judge me.

1 Preheat the oven to 200°C fan (425°F/Gas mark 7). Boil the spaghetti according to the packet instructions. Please, for the love of god, salt your pasta water like it's the ocean! I like to pull the pasta out 1 minute early because it will continue to cook in the sauce. Make sure you also reserve some of the pasta water as it's liquid gold.

2 Pat the salmon dry and place on a tray lined with baking parchment. Drizzle with the oil, massage it in and season with the lemon pepper seasoning and chilli flakes.

3 Bake for about 7 minutes, ideally when it reaches an internal temperature of 50–55°C (122–131°F). Allow to rest for 3–5 minutes.

4 While the salmon is cooking, prepare the sauce. Add the butter to a pan over medium heat and, once melted, bang in the shallot, garlic and thyme. Cook for 2–3 minutes – the shallot and garlic shouldn't be gaining any colour. If they are, you need to drop the heat.

5 Now add the cream and lemon juice and simmer over medium heat for 5 minutes, or until the sauce has thickened and can coat the back of a spoon.

6 Add the lemon zest, dill, salt and pepper and stir until incorporated. At this point you can drop the heat to low as the sauce is done. Adjust the seasoning if necessary; however, I don't think you'll need to, but it's important to taste as you cook.

7 Flake one of your salmon fillets into the sauce, keeping it quite chunky. Add the pasta and get it coated in that glorious sauce. If you find it isn't saucy enough, add a splash of the reserved pasta water to loosen it up.

8 Finally, serve with a few broken-up chunks of the remaining salmon and a sprinkle of pepper and dill.

JAMAICAN OXTAIL

SERVES 4–6

1.5 kg (3 lb 5 oz) oxtail, cut into
  2–3 cm (1–1¼ inch) thick rounds
2–3 tablespoons oil
1½ tablespoons soft brown sugar
1½ Scotch bonnet peppers: 1 left
  whole, ½ minced
½ onion, diced
1 carrot, peeled and sliced into 5 mm
  (¼ inch) rounds
1 bell pepper (capsicum), a mix of
  yellow and green, diced
6–8 sprigs of fresh thyme
3 spring onions (scallions), sliced
2 bay leaves
3 tablespoons ketchup
3–4 tablespoons dark soy sauce
400 g (14 oz) tin butter (lima)
  beans, drained

Marinade
1 tablespoon salt
2 teaspoons all-purpose seasoning
2 teaspoons dark brown sugar
1 teaspoon ground allspice
5 pimento berries
1½ tablespoons minced garlic
1½ tablespoons minced fresh ginger
4 tablespoons Green Seasoning
  (page 200)
2 teaspoons browning

THIS OXTAIL IS A SUNDAY DINNER FAVOURITE. I can vividly remember the smell of it bubbling away when I was younger and stealing the smallest pieces from the pot so it would go undetected. Well, that's what I thought, but I can confirm my mum definitely knew. This is proper comfort food — if I'm feeling down, a good plate of this with some plantain, coleslaw and rice gets me right and going again. For me, it's just happiness in a bowl.

Growing up this was definitely a treat meal, something that I appreciated even more once I learned how to cook it myself. It might seem a little overwhelming but, trust me, it's extremely easy and it's definitely worth the wait. You can speed up the cooking process by using a pressure cooker or you can keep it old school and make it on the hob. I prefer the hob method because you really can't beat low and slow cooking. It's definitely more cost effective to bang it in the pressure cooker, though. Now, when it comes to cooking meat in any stew, you never want to add cold water to your pot. Always use hot water or you'll make the meat tense up, which is what my mum always used to say to me growing up.

As in a lot of Jamaican food, meat like oxtail, which is considered a luxurious cut to most now, was once considered a scrap cut. I highly recommend getting your butcher to trim the extra fat for you, these days most of the oxtail I buy needs minimal trimming. If you need to trim your oxtail yourself, then you ideally want to leave around 5 mm (¼ inch) of fat max, like a little outline around the oxtail which keeps it moist like a blanket! Fat = FLAYVA. However, anything more than this won't render down and will just have a horrible mouthfeel. The price of oxtail is rising, so that means you need a certified recipe that won't let you down. This is that recipe — you're welcome.

continued overleaf

1   Pat the oxtail dry and season with all the marinade ingredients. Cover and allow to marinate in the refrigerator overnight for best results, or for a few hours. Two hours is better than no hours.

2   Heat a pot over medium–high heat, add the oil and brown sugar and cook for 1–2 minutes. Stir carefully as it dissolves; it might get a little smoky but that's fine! Once it's bubbling, it's ready.

3   Add the oxtail pieces into the pot. Cook over medium heat for 10 minutes, or until nice and browned on all sides. Ensure you're turning them often so they don't burn.

4   Now, add the minced Scotch bonnet pepper, onion, carrot, pepper, thyme, spring onions and bay leaves. Give it a mix, cover and cook over low–medium heat for 3–5 minutes. This will release the natural waters within the veg.

5   Cover with enough hot water to keep the meat submerged. There should be no more than 2.5 cm (1 inch) of water above the meat during this part of the cooking process. Place on the lid and cook over low–medium heat for about 3 hours.

6   Cooking times will vary depending on the size of the oxtail, so check after the 2½ hours and continue to add hot water to keep the meat covered. Oxtail tends to be quite fatty, so you'll see something that resembles the consistency of oil sitting at the top. You want to skim the fat from the surface with a large spoon as the meat cooks. If using a pressure cooker, cook on high for 1 hour, then move to the hob for the next step.

7   Add the ketchup, soy sauce and butter beans. Stir until incorporated, then add the whole Scotch bonnet pepper and cook, partially covered, for 15–30 minutes. This will also allow the sauce to thicken.

8   Once done, the meat should be tender and pull away with a fork. Serve with white rice, plantain and coleslaw.

JERK CHICKEN

8 skin-on chicken legs
350–400 g (12–14 oz) Wet Jerk
 Marinade (page 207)
1 tablespoon all-purpose seasoning

Lager–spiked honey jerk ketchup
250 g (9 oz) ketchup
200 ml (7 fl oz) Jamaican lager
150 ml (5 fl oz) chicken stock
 (reduced sodium)
200 g (7 oz) honey
juice of 1 lime, plus zest of ½
1–2 tablespoons leftover jerk
 marinade

BBQ method (optional)
2 large handfuls of pimento leaves,
 soaked in water for 1 hour
3 tablespoons pimento (allspice)
 berries, soaked in water for 1 hour
200 ml (7 fl oz) Jamaican lager

Oven method (optional)
200 ml (7 fl oz) chicken stock
 or water

When people think of Jamaican food, this is the dish a lot of people think of first. Funnily enough, jerk chicken is NOT the national dish of Jamaica, but the flayvas are so bold and renowned that I can understand why it is people's first thought. I often hear people say jerk chicken is overrated but I'm here to tell you these people are wild! If you've had the pleasure of tasting proper jerk chicken, then you'll know it's worth all the hype, plus tax!

Jerk chicken is a popular Jamaican dish that is known for its aromatic and spicy flavours. The dish dates back to my ancestors from the Maroon tribe, runaway enslaved people who lived in the hills of Jamaica during the 17th century. They created the dish by mixing a variety of spices and rubbing them onto the meat, which was then cooked slowly over a fire pit in the ground so they would go undetected, as it released minimal smoke. The result is a dish which is a perfect combination of smoky, tender and fall–off–the–bone meat. For those reasons alone it's solidified its place as a popular go–to for many people.

Jerk chicken is traditionally cooked on a grill over pimento wood and coal, which gives it that distinctive smoky flavour. The perfect jerk chicken for me has to get a slight smoke ring. I like to let mine cook on the BBQ and really soak up that smoke because it honestly penetrates right to the bone. Jerk chicken isn't jerk chicken without some sweet jerk–spiced ketchup — it's zingy, it's sweet and it just adds an extra layer of love to this meat.

This delicious dish has gained so much popularity all over the world and is often served at BBQs, parties and family gatherings. So, fire up your grill and get ready to experience my take on the mouthwatering flayvas of jerk chicken.

continued overleaf

BBQ METHOD

1 Pat the chicken legs dry, then poke carefully with a knife to create some holes. Season with the wet jerk marinade and all-purpose seasoning, carefully separating the skin from the legs to get it all up in there! Cover and leave to marinate in the refrigerator for at least 24 hours or up to 48 hours.

2 Remove the chicken from the refrigerator and allow it to sit at room temperature for 30 minutes.

3 Prepare a charcoal grill (with a lid) for indirect cooking – this means you want your coals on one side and the other side to have no coal under the grates where your meat will sit. You're looking for a temperature of 150–160°C (300–320°F) and the majority of your coals should be white. You can cook at a higher temperature, but I personally prefer more of a low and slow method. **You don't want too much coal as you will 'bun up the chicken', as my grandad would say.** You can add coal later to maintain the temperature.

4 Now oil your grates. Opposite the coals you want to create a layer using two-thirds of the soaked pimento leaves and a few of the pimento berries; it's fine if some fall through the grates. You essentially want the leaves as a bed for the chicken. Shake off the excess marinade from the chicken and place skin-side up on the leaves. Close the lid and leave to cook for 15–20 minutes. You want your top vents completely open and bottom/side vents half to two-thirds open.

5 While the chicken is cooking, spray it with lager every 15–20 minutes to keep it nice and moist.

6 To prepare the lager-spiked honey jerk ketchup, put all the ingredients in a pan, bring to the boil and simmer over medium heat until it can coat the back of a spoon.

7 Open the BBQ lid, rotate the chicken pieces so that the ones closest to the coals are now on the opposite side. Check if you need to add more coal to maintain the heat, then place the remaining pimento leaves on the hot side of the grill – it's going to get smoky! Close and cook for another 15–20 minutes.

8 Now rotate the chicken again, give it another spray of lager, dash your remaining berries directly onto the coals and cook until the thickest part of the chicken has an internal temperature of 80°C (165°F).

9   Once the chicken is at 80°C (165°F), spray it once more with lager and place directly over the coals to gain some colour and char. You're going to want to turn the chicken regularly because it is cooked at this point. Once the chicken reaches an internal temperature of 84°C (185°F) and has gained some nice bits of char, pull it off the heat. You can also leave the chicken on the indirect side with no coals if you want to keep it warm. Some people like to brush their chicken with some of the lager-spiked sauce at this point, but that's optional.

10 Allow the chicken to rest for 5–10 minutes before chopping your legs into 4–5 pieces with a cleaver. Serve with plantain, rice and peas, coleslaw and lashings of your lager-spiked sauce.

OVEN METHOD

1   Follow steps 1–2 of the BBQ method.

2   Preheat the oven to 180°C fan (400°F/Gas mark 6). Place your chicken legs on a tray lined with baking parchment or foil, then add your chicken stock, but don't pour the chicken stock directly on the chicken, as this will wash away the flayvas!

3   Cover with foil and roast for 25–30 minutes, then remove the foil and baste the chicken. Reduce the temperature to 160°C fan (350°F/Gas mark 4). Insert a wire rack onto your tray, place the chicken legs on top and roast for another 30–45 minutes, checking regularly and basting with juices from the pan.

4   Follow step 6 of the BBQ method to make the lager-spiked honey jerk ketchup.

5   Once the chicken reaches an internal temperature of 84°C (185°F), remove from the oven and allow to rest for 5–10 minutes. Then serve up in the same style as the BBQ method.

FLAYVAFUL POT ROAST

SERVES 6

1.4 kg (3 lb 2 oz) boneless beef
   chuck roast or beef roast joint, such
   as brisket (brisket may take slightly
   longer to cook)
2 tablespoons vegetable oil
5 carrots: 2 finely diced, 3 peeled
   and chopped into 4 cm (1½ inch)
   chunks
2 ribs of celery, finely diced
2 onions: 1 diced, 1 roughly sliced
8 garlic cloves, minced
175 ml (6 fl oz) dry red wine
500 ml–1 litre (17–35 fl oz)
   reduced-sodium beef stock
1½ tablespoons beef stock paste or
   1 beef stock cube
2 tablespoons ketchup
1½ tablespoons dark soy sauce
1 tablespoon dark soft brown sugar
2 tablespoons Worcestershire sauce
3 sprigs of fresh thyme
3 sprigs of fresh rosemary
2 bay leaves
850 g (1 lb 14 oz) waxy potatoes,
   such as red potatoes, cut into 4 cm
   (1½ inch) chunks
2 tablespoons cornflour (cornstarch),
   mixed with 4 tablespoons water
salt and pepper
chopped fresh parsley, to serve

Slow-cooked, mouthwatering caramelised onion and beef chuck roast. Now, a beef roast is an absolute classic, but my god, do some of them need some love! A sad beef roast? Yeah, no thanks. It's a big no from me! This one really is so easy to make, packed with flayvas, a super-rich gravy and crazily tender meat. This slow-cooked recipe is the perfect choice for a hearty meal that requires minimal effort. Beef chuck is a notoriously tough cut of meat, but when you cook it nice and slow and let that tissue and fat break down you're left in meat heaven.

One of the key parts of this recipe is the gravy — that really makes or breaks a roast for me. So we build depth and flavour in the initial steps of this recipe. When choosing your chuck roast, you want one that's marbled with fat because that's where the flayvas are at! Once that fat breaks down between each grain of meat it's like soft buttery goodness. You can also use a beef brisket roast, but this may take slightly longer to cook.

Even if you slow cook this using a slow cooker, you still need to sear the beef. Searing the beef and creating a crust creates more FLAYVAS. And that's what I'm all about.

1 Preheat the oven to 140°C fan (325°F/Gas mark 3).

2 Alright, you want to pat the beef dry, then season very generously with salt and some pepper on all sides. It's really important that you pat the beef dry, as this ensures we get a great sear! When I say generously season, you want it to be evenly coated, just like a steak.

3 Then, over high heat in a large pot or Dutch oven, add the oil and sear the beef on all sides, or until a golden crust has formed. This should take about 2 minutes per side. Then pop the beef to the side.

4 Drop the heat to low-medium and cook off the finely diced carrots, celery and all the onions. Cook for 4 minutes, then add the garlic and cook for a further minute. After 5 minutes everything should have started to soften.

5 Deglaze the pot with the red wine and really scrape up all those flayvas off the bottom. Allow to reduce for 2–3 minutes, then add 500 ml (17 fl oz) beef stock, the beef stock paste, ketchup, soy sauce, brown sugar and Worcestershire sauce. Mix until combined, then add the thyme, rosemary and bay leaves.

6 Add the beef and make sure your aromatics are nestled in too. You need enough stock to submerge the beef, so top up with more beef stock if needed.

7 Cover and roast for 2 hours, then add the potatoes and chopped carrots, sprinkle with salt and pepper and roast for another 1–1¾ hours, or until the meat is tender.

8 If you are using a slow cooker, add the beef to the bottom, then add the beef cooking juices, potatoes and carrots. Top up with more stock if needed. Slow cook on low for 8–9 hours. Then follow step 9 onwards.

9 Once tender, remove the beef from the pot, use a slotted spoon to remove the potatoes and carrots and place to rest on the side, covered, while you prepare your gravy.

10 Skim any fat from the surface of the pot and discard. You can strain the juices or keep the little chunks in, but you're going to want to thicken the gravy with your cornflour mixture.

11 Place the pot over medium heat, add half the cornflour mixture and stir. The amount you need will completely depend on the size of your pot and how much liquid is left, so I recommend starting with half. If for some reason you don't have much cooking liquid left, top up with more beef stock. Then add the remaining cornflour mixture until you get your desired thickness of gravy.

12 Tear the beef into large chunks and serve on a serving tray with the carrots, potatoes, drizzles of gravy and freshly chopped parsley to finish.

LEMON, THYME & GARLIC BUTTER BAKED COD

SERVES 2–4

6 cod fillets
4 tablespoons butter, melted
2 teaspoons fresh lemon juice
3 garlic cloves, minced
2 teaspoons fresh thyme leaves
½ teaspoon cayenne pepper
1 teaspoon chilli flakes
2 tablespoons olive oil
2–3 teaspoons Lemon Pepper
  Seasoning (page 201)
5 tablespoons fish or vegetable stock
Creamy Garlic Mash (page 103),
  to serve

To garnish
lemon slices
chopped fresh parsley

ANOTHER MIDWEEK FLAYVAS BANGER. A lot of people shy away from cooking cod because they don't want it to be bland and dry — that's a double whammy of sadness. I'll be honest, outside of my own cooking, if it's not miso black cod or fish and chips, I'm not really interested because a lot of places just don't create wow-tasting cod. It's the little things that make a difference.

I've developed this recipe for ease, but most important of all... flayvas. Quick, but easy flayvas that no one can mess up. This is one of those dishes that will boost your confidence in the kitchen and allow you to find your own flair. **This is another recipe I use when I just want something a little lighter for dinner. I like to use a cast-iron or oven-safe pan as it saves me using two dishes. I've also included an oven-only version because I love you and care for your time!**

1 Preheat the oven to 200°C fan (425°F/Gas mark 7). Leave the cod fillets at room temperature for 15–20 minutes – this will enable the fish to cook evenly.

2 In a small bowl, whisk together the melted butter, lemon juice, garlic, thyme, cayenne pepper and chilli flakes. Pop to the side – we will need this later.

3 Pat the cod fillets dry to remove any excess moisture from the surface, as we're going to sear them in the pan. Drizzle with 1 tablespoon of the olive oil and season with the lemon pepper seasoning; the amount you'll need will vary depending on the surface area of your cod. They should be evenly coated.

4 Put an oven-safe pan over medium heat, add the remaining tablespoon of oil and sear the cod fillets for 1 minute per side. This is just to lock in some flayva!

5 Remove from the heat and add the fish stock to deglaze the pan. Spoon the butter mixture over the cod fillets.

6 Bang in the oven and bake for 10 minutes, or until the fish is cooked through and flakes easily with a fork. Allow to rest for 2–3 minutes.

7 Garnish the cod fillets with lemon slices and chopped parsley.

continued overleaf

OVEN–ONLY METHOD

1 Preheat the oven to 200°C fan (425°F/Gas mark 7). Ensure your cod fillets are sitting at room temperature for 15–20 minutes. This will enable the fish to cook evenly.

2 Pat the cod fillets dry, drizzle with 1 tablespoon of olive oil and season with the lemon pepper seasoning. Place them in an oven-safe dish, ensuring they are not touching as you don't want to overcrowd the dish and slow down the cooking process.

3 In a small bowl, whisk together the melted butter, lemon juice, garlic, thyme, cayenne pepper, chilli flakes and fish stock.

4 Spoon the butter mixture over the cod fillets and bang in the oven for 10–12 minutes, or until the fish is cooked through and flakes easily with a fork. Allow to rest for 2–3 minutes.

5 Garnish the cod fillets with lemon slices and chopped parsley. Serve with creamy garlic mash.

PIMENTO-SPICED TACOS

Juicy tacos with a fruity, citrusy pico de gallo, a little bit of cheese and lots and lots of love. One of the best things that came out of me moving to London was learning about Mexican cuisine. I've had the pleasure of working with a few Mexican chefs who really helped me learn about the culture, including making my own corn tortillas and understanding chillies and their uses. I'm a sucker for tacos and I'm ALWAYS in the mood for them. When it comes to tacos, I really do appreciate a crispy one. It just tastes so much better! I'm a textures person when it comes to food, so a lot of the time when I'm creating and developing recipes, I'm thinking of the elements I would improve or the elements I don't like, so I can make them work better.

This recipe is another fusion one, but it's pretty subtle. The pimento isn't crazily overpowering but it's present and it's really such a beautiful touch. I love the role that pimento plays in jerk chicken, which is why I add just enough for it to almost become the main character. Corn tortillas really make a difference because they get lovely and crispy. You can use flour ones too, but you won't get that same crunch.

SERVES 4

6 boneless and skinless chicken
  thighs (600 g/1 lb 5 oz)
1 tablespoon dried oregano
2 teaspoons ground allspice
1 teaspoon all-purpose seasoning
2–3 tablespoons vegetable oil
350 ml (12 fl oz) reduced-sodium
  chicken stock
12–14 x 12 cm (4½ inch) corn tortillas
200 g (7 oz) smoked or regular
  mozzarella, grated

Marinade
½ red bell pepper (capsicum)
½ onion
5 garlic cloves, peeled
2 tablespoons Wet Jerk Marinade
  (page 207)
1 tablespoon olive oil
2 tablespoons dark soft brown sugar
1 tablespoon pimento (allspice)
  berries
1 tablespoon dried oregano
1 teaspoon ground cumin
juice of 1 lime
2 teaspoons salt

Pico de gallo
2 large tomatoes, deseeded
  and diced
4 tablespoons diced pineapple
½ red onion, diced
¼ Scotch bonnet pepper, deseeded
  and diced
2 tablespoons chopped fresh
  coriander (cilantro)
juice of 1 lime
½ teaspoon black pepper
½ teaspoon salt

1   Preheat the oven to 210°C fan (450°F/Gas mark 8).

2   Alright, so the first thing you want to do is roast the red pepper, onion and garlic for 5–10 minutes, or until you start to see some char.

3   Once it's cooled, add your roasted veg to a blender and blitz with the wet jerk marinade, olive oil, brown sugar, pimento berries, oregano, cumin, lime juice and salt.

4   Season the chicken thighs with the oregano, allspice and all-purpose seasoning. Rub that in, pour over your marinade and mix. Cover and marinate in the refrigerator overnight, or for at least a few hours.

5   While the chicken marinates, combine all the pico de gallo ingredients in a bowl and mix together. I find it tastes best when you let it sit in the refrigerator for 1 hour.

6   Preheat a pan over medium–high heat. Once hot, add 1½ tablespoons of vegetable oil and shake or wipe off a bit of the excess marinade. You don't want too much marinade on the chicken as you sear it because too much of the marinade will burn.

7   Flip after 3–4 minutes, then cook over medium heat for another 3 minutes. Add the chicken stock and simmer over low–medium heat for 10 minutes. The chicken should have an internal temperature of 78–82°C (170–180°F).

8   Let your chicken rest for 5 minutes, then chop into small chunks.

9   Now, in a clean pan over low–medium heat, add a little more oil, then add your corn tortillas, a sprinkle of mozzarella and some chopped chicken; you only need about 1–2 tablespoons of chicken and a tiny bit of cheese. Carefully fold over and seal your tacos and allow to cook for 1–2 minutes per side until crispy. Keep warm on a tray in the oven at 80°C (175°F) while you build your remaining tacos.

10 To serve your tacos, open them up to expose that cheesy goodness and add a good amount of your fruity pico de gallo.

CURRIED BUTTER BEANS
& CRISPY HERB CHICKEN

SERVES 2–4

2–3 tablespoons coconut oil
1 medium onion, diced
1 tablespoon minced garlic
1 teaspoon minced fresh ginger
¼ Scotch bonnet pepper, minced
2 teaspoons fresh thyme leaves
1 tablespoon curry powder
1 teaspoon garam masala
1 teaspoon all-purpose seasoning
1 tablespoon ground cumin
2 x 400 g (14 oz) tins of butter
  (lima) beans, drained
3 teaspoons salt
300 ml (10½ fl oz) oat milk
100 ml (3½ fl oz) chicken stock
6 skin-on, boneless chicken thighs
1 teaspoon black pepper
1 teaspoon all-purpose seasoning
1 teaspoon smoked paprika
2 garlic cloves, minced
2 sprigs of fresh thyme

To garnish
chopped fresh coriander (cilantro)
sliced red chillies

This is the type of recipe you make midweek, when you've been having a busy week but crave something comforting, which will make your belly feel warm inside but takes minimal effort. For me, the best pieces of chicken are thighs and they're one of the cheaper, tastier and most forgiving cuts of meat. They really take this recipe to the next level. I like to use skin-on, boneless chicken thighs for this recipe — the skin is crispy, and thighs are the tastiest part of the chicken after the wings. Boneless thighs also take a whole lot less time to cook; you could use bone-in thighs but I would recommend finishing them in the oven. Trust me when I say that all your chicken skin needs is salt when you're pan-searing it. Pan-searing chicken is a completely different ball game to roasting, and one that requires skill. Repeat after me: any other seasoning burns! I know it might be quite hard to believe that I only use salt on the skin, but that's the secret to crispy chicken. Don't get it twisted though, we do also season the flesh side!

I really like to add curry powder to my butter beans, as it's just a nice, warm, earthy taste that only a mad person couldn't love... well, that's what I think anyway. I like that you can really control the spice with this one and if you don't want spice, it doesn't negatively impact the dish in any way.

1   The first thing you want to start on is the curried butter beans. In a pan over medium heat, add the coconut oil, starting with 2 tablespoons. Add the onion, garlic, ginger and Scotch bonnet. Cook for 2–3 minutes or until nice and softened. At this point there shouldn't be any colour.

2   Next, add the thyme, curry powder, garam masala, all-purpose seasoning and cumin. Stir continuously for 2–3 minutes and allow those spices to really infuse and create a beautiful flayva base. If you find that it's dry and a paste hasn't formed, add the remaining tablespoon of coconut oil.

3   Now bang in your drained butter beans, season with 1 teaspoon of salt and get them coated in all that goodness for a minute before adding the oat milk and chicken stock. Cook for 10–15 minutes over low–medium heat, stirring every now and then.

4   For the chicken thighs, pat them dry to remove any excess moisture from the skin. Season the flesh side with about 1½ teaspoons of salt, the pepper, all-purpose seasoning and paprika. Carefully turn over and brush off any seasoning that may have got on the skin. Season the skin with the remaining salt. Season from 20 cm (8 inches) above the chicken for even coverage. The amount of salt you'll need will vary depending on the size of your chicken thighs: if you have small thighs, then use around one-third less salt. Ultimately, the aim is for the chicken skin to be evenly coated in salt, just like a steak. Think of the salt as icing (confectioners') sugar – you want to dust it like that!

5   Place your chicken thighs skin-side down in a cold pan, preferably cast iron. Gradually increase the heat to medium over the course of 3–5 minutes. This will allow the chicken to cook slowly and render out the fat. Once you get to medium heat, allow your chicken to sizzle away for another 8–10 minutes, or until the skin is golden (check every few minutes!). Once golden, flip your chicken, drop the heat to low and add your minced garlic and thyme and baste with the chicken fat that's been produced in the pan. The total cooking time should be about 14–16 minutes, or your thighs should read 77–82°C (171–180°F). Chicken thighs are still juicy yet tender at this temperature, but you can cook them to 74°C (165°F) if you prefer.

6   Let the chicken thighs rest for 5 minutes before tearing them into chunks. At this point your beans should be done; if they're a little dry, loosen up with oat milk or water. Serve the chicken over the curried butter beans. Garnish with coriander and sliced red chilli.

HERB ROASTED LAMB

SERVES 6—8

1.5–1.8 kg (3 lb 5 oz–4 lb) bone-in
  lamb shoulder
1 tablespoon olive oil
about 1½–2 tablespoons Herb Salt
  (page 210)
3–4 teaspoons all-purpose seasoning
5–6 garlic cloves, halved
6 sprigs of fresh rosemary
2 onions
1 bulb of garlic
500 ml (17 fl oz) reduced-sodium
  beef or vegetable stock
200–450 ml (7–16 fl oz) water
5 tablespoons mint sauce
5 tablespoons honey

Gravy

4 tablespoons plain (all-purpose)
  flour
175 ml (5½ fl oz) red wine
700 ml (24 fl oz) reduced-sodium
  beef stock
½–1 teaspoon gravy browning

SLOW-ROASTED LAMB? You can't really mess it up and it requires less skill than cooking lamb to that restaurant-style blushing pink. I've not met many people who haven't liked slow-cooked tender lamb that's slightly sticky and just so moreish. Lamb is one of those meats that soaks up flavvas so well, but at the same time you can keep it simple, and it will still taste beautiful. I prefer lamb shoulder because it's less lean and has a better flavva throughout.

The whole point of this recipe is to teach you how to master the basics and take some risks with your cooking. **This recipe is really a base recipe. With the timings, temperature and method listed here, you'll always get a perfect result, but you can always switch up the seasoning as you get more confident with your cooking. With recipes like this, the salt will vary because not every piece of lamb is the same, some have a greater surface area than others. You want to generously season your lamb with salt though; think of it as a steak. This is my rule when it comes to using salt on meat and if that isn't really clear, think of the salt as icing (confectioners') sugar that you want to evenly dust over the meat.**

1   Preheat the oven to 200°C fan (425°F/Gas mark 7). While the oven is heating up, remove the lamb from the refrigerator and allow it to sit at room temperature for 45 minutes.

2   Drizzle the olive oil over the lamb and really massage it in. Then generously season the lamb with the herb salt and all-purpose seasoning, ensuring every nook and cranny has salt. Remember this is a big joint of meat. Make about 10–12 incisions in the lamb and insert the garlic clove halves along with some of the rosemary broken into little bits; make sure it's completely stuffed in the joint so it doesn't burn. I love this part because once the lamb is done, the garlic almost confits as it cooks within the lamb and its juices.

3   Slice the onions and garlic bulb in half and make a nice cosy little bed for your lamb. Place the lamb, shoulder-side up, on the onions and garlic and add the stock and water directly to the tray and not over the lamb, otherwise you're just washing all that seasoning AWAY!

4   Tightly wrap with foil, but ensure the foil isn't touching the lamb. Make sure you create a tight seal as we don't want any of the juices to escape. Double wrap with foil if needed, or roast with a lid. Roast for 30 minutes, then reduce the temperature to 150°C fan (340°F/Gas mark 3½) and roast for a further 2½ hours.

continued overleaf

5   After 3 hours of roasting, remove the foil and coat the lamb in the cooking juices. Mix together the mint sauce and honey and brush over the lamb, then pour over a spoon or two of the cooking juices. If you find there are barely any juices in the pan, add another 250 ml (9 fl oz) stock or water. Increase the temperature to 200°C fan (425°F/Gas mark 7) and roast for 25 minutes to gain some colour. Remove from the oven and allow to rest for 30 minutes.

6   Now, using a sieve, drain the remaining cooking juices into a pot and add the flour. Whisk continuously over medium–high heat. Once a gravy has formed, add the red wine and beef stock and simmer for 10–15 minutes over low heat. If you find that your gravy is too thick, add a little more stock or water. The amount of cooking juices you have will completely vary, so you'll need to play around with adding stock or water.

7   Reduce over medium heat for 5–7 minutes, or until you've reached your desired thickness. Then add the gravy browning and it's done! Now, you should have no lumps, but if you do, simply strain it and you're good to go.

8   Tear the lamb and serve with lashings of gravy. I LOVE having this lamb with gratin potatoes (page 119).

ACKEE CURRY

SERVES 4

3 green plantains
540 g (1 lb 3 oz) tin ackee
2 tablespoons coconut oil
2 teaspoons cumin seeds
1 teaspoon fennel seeds
1 medium onion, finely diced
1 tablespoon minced garlic
1 teaspoon minced fresh ginger
1 teaspoon fresh thyme leaves
1 tablespoon curry powder
1 teaspoon ground fenugreek
1 teaspoon ground allspice
1 teaspoon ground cinnamon
½ teaspoon ground turmeric
2 large tomatoes, diced
1 red bell pepper (capsicum),
  medium diced
2 spring onions (scallions), sliced
½ Scotch bonnet pepper, minced
  with or without seeds (seeds
  add spice)
500 g (1 lb 2 oz) peeled red
  potatoes, cut into 2 cm
  (¾ inch) cubes
400 ml (14 fl oz) coconut milk
½ teaspoon black pepper
vegetable oil, for frying
salt

BACK AGAIN WITH SOME VEGAN GOODNESS. **This ackee curry is rich, creamy, spicy and full-bodied with flayvas. I'll tell you for free that it's sensational. Ackee is so versatile, you just need to understand how to use it. Remember, if you strip food down to its flavour profile and textures it makes taking risks so much simpler. To me, ackee is creamy, kinda nutty, kinda buttery and melts in your mouth. All those things sound like what I would want and love in a curry. Ackee costs an arm and a leg, so trust me, I would never give you a recipe I wasn't sure of! I've tried and tested this baby and it never ever comes up short.**

I keep this one simple and serve it with some plantain chips to scoop up all that creamy curry goodness. It can be enjoyed as a main or as a side dish dip, which I really do enjoy the most. **You want to use a mandoline (with a guard, of course!) for the plantain chips, as it's the only way you'll achieve that crispy straight-out-of-the-packet effect.**

1   To make the plantain crisps, peel and thinly slice the plantains with a mandoline. Cover the plantains with ice-cold water until fully submerged and season with 2 teaspoons of salt – this will preserve the plantain and stop it turning brown and it will also firm up the plantain, which makes it easier to handle when frying.

2   Drain your ackee in a sieve or colander and leave it suspended over a bowl to catch any excess moisture. Be careful though as ackee is very delicate.

3   In a pan over medium heat, add the coconut oil and, once melted and hot, toast the cumin and fennel seeds for a minute, then add the onion, garlic, ginger and thyme. Cook over medium heat for 1–2 minutes, or until the onion has started to soften. **It should smell fragrant!**

4   Add the curry powder, fenugreek, allspice, cinnamon and turmeric. Allow the spices to cook for a few minutes over low–medium heat, stirring constantly to ensure the onion and garlic aren't burning.

5   Get all those flayvas acquainted, then add the tomatoes, red pepper, spring onions and Scotch bonnet pepper. Cook for 2–3 minutes until the tomatoes start to break down and form a paste-like sauce.

6   Mix in the potatoes and coconut milk, then cook on a rolling simmer for 20–25 minutes. Once the potatoes are completely cooked through, add the ackee and carefully fold in to incorporate all the ingredients. Simmer over medium heat, uncovered, for 3–5 minutes. Add salt to taste along with the black pepper.

7   Heat about 7.5–10 cm (3–4 inches) of oil in a heavy-bottomed deep pan to 180°C (350°F), shake any excess water off the plantain and fry for 1–2 minutes, or until golden and crispy. **Ensure you fry in batches as you don't want to overcrowd the oil and drop the temperature.** Place on kitchen paper to drain any excess oil. Sprinkle them with salt while hot.

8   Serve the curried ackee with the plantain chips and dig in.

BEEF SHIN CHILLI LASAGNE

750 g (1 lb 10 oz) boneless beef shin, diced into 5 cm (2 inch) chunks
3–4 tablespoons vegetable oil
2 teaspoons cumin seeds
2 teaspoons fennel seeds
2 teaspoons coriander seeds
2 large carrots, peeled and finely diced
2 ribs of celery, finely diced
2 large onions, finely diced
7 garlic cloves, minced
2 tablespoons tomato paste (concentrated purée)
5 tablespoons harissa paste
1 teaspoon cayenne pepper
1 teaspoon smoked paprika
1 teaspoon chilli flakes
1 teaspoon all-purpose seasoning
150 ml (5 fl oz) red wine or 4 tablespoons balsamic vinegar
300 ml (10½ fl oz) beef stock
400 g (14 oz) tin chopped tomatoes
300 g (10½ oz) tomato passata (puréed tomatoes)
8 fresh basil leaves, roughly chopped
250–300 g (9–10½ oz) fresh or dried lasagne sheets
Italian or mixed herbs, for topping
salt

Béchamel
6 tablespoons butter
7 tablespoons plain (all-purpose) flour
1 litre (35 fl oz) full-fat milk
150 g (5½ oz) soft garlic and herb cheese
250 g (9 oz) Gruyère, grated
1½ teaspoons freshly grated nutmeg
½ teaspoon salt
1 teaspoon black pepper
200 g (7 oz) mozzarella
100 g (3½ oz) Parmesan

OH, I HOPE YOU'RE READY FOR THIS LASAGNE. **Packed with bold flavours, it's the perfect combination of tender, slightly spicy beef and rich tomato sauce. Now, the key to my béchamel sauce is a creamy garlic soft cheese. One thing about me? I love me some garlic!**

To add a little fusion spin to this classic Italian dish, I've incorporated harissa paste, a North African spice blend, which adds a depth and complexity and makes you wonder why you didn't do it before. The beef shin is cooked low and slow until it becomes melt–in–your–mouth tender, making it the perfect filling for this lasagne. The slight kick of heat from the chilli is balanced with the sweetness of the tomato sauce, creating a perfect harmony of flayvas.

This lasagne is also a satisfying and comforting dish that's perfect for family dinners or meal prepping. **You're really going to enjoy it when you tuck into this unique and delicious take on lasagne that's sure to impress. It doesn't even matter if you have leftover meat because it can be enjoyed with spaghetti later on in the week. It really is a win–win recipe.**

1   Pat the beef shin chunks dry with kitchen paper and season generously with salt – you need just enough to lightly dust the meat.

2   In a large pot or Dutch oven, heat the oil over medium–high heat. Once the oil is hot, I'm talking burn-your-fingertips-off hot, add the beef shin chunks in a single layer and sear for 2–3 minutes on each side until browned. Work in batches if necessary to avoid overcrowding the pot. Remove the beef from the pot and set it aside.

3   In the same pot, reduce the heat to low–medium and toast the cumin, fennel and coriander seeds for a minute or two until fragrant. Then add the carrots, celery, onions and garlic and cook over medium heat for 5–7 minutes until softened and slightly browned, stirring occasionally.

4   Stir in the tomato paste, harissa paste, cayenne pepper, smoked paprika, chilli flakes and all-purpose seasoning until combined. Cook for another minute or two.

5   Then add the red wine and beef stock to deglaze the pan, which is just the cheffy way of saying catch all the flayvas that are stuck to the bottom! Really stir to catch everything, then add the seared beef chunks (plus any resting juices), pour in the chopped tomatoes and passata and stir to combine. Bring to the boil, then add the basil leaves.

continued overleaf

6   Cover and simmer over low heat for 2–2½ hours until the beef is tender and can shred.

7   While the beef is simmering, prepare the béchamel sauce. Melt the butter in a saucepan over medium heat. Add the flour and whisk until smooth. Cook for 2–3 minutes until lightly golden, then gradually whisk in the milk until the mixture thickens. Be sure to use a spatula to catch the bottom of the pot so it doesn't burn.

8   Turn off the heat, stir in the soft cheese and 200 g (7 oz) of the Gruyère until melted, then season with the nutmeg, salt and pepper. Continue to stir until the sauce is smooth. At this point I like to grate my mozzarella, Parmesan and remaining 50 g (1¾ oz) Gruyère for the topping. I also like to use the rinds from the Gruyère and Parmesan and place them in the pot with the beef. No flayvas are wasted!

9   Once your meat is done, shred with a fork and if your sauce isn't thick yet, then allow to simmer, uncovered, over medium heat until your mixture has thickened like a ragù. Once done, check the seasoning and adjust with salt or pepper as needed, and remove the cheese rinds.

10 If using dried pasta sheets, bring a large pot of water to the boil. You'll need 1 litre (35 fl oz) of water for every 100 g (3½ oz) of pasta. Bring to the boil with plenty of salt and blanch the pasta sheets in batches for 3–4 minutes so they don't stick, then proceed to the next step.

11 Preheat the oven to 180°C fan (400°F/Gas mark 6).

12 Assemble the lasagne in a 25 x 30 cm (9 x 12 inch) dish. Start by spreading a very small layer of beef shin mixture on the bottom – this stops your lasagne sheets from sticking. Then cover with a layer of fresh or cooked lasagne sheets, enough meat sauce so you can't really see the pasta sheets, a layer of the béchamel sauce on top and a sprinkle of Parmesan and mozzarella. Repeat this layering process until all the ingredients are used up, ending with a layer of béchamel sauce topped with grated Gruyère, Parmesan and mozzarella and a sprinkle of Italian herbs to top.

13 Cover with foil and bake for 20 minutes (ensure the foil isn't touching the top), then remove the foil and cook for a further 15 minutes, or until golden.

14 Allow the lasagne to cool and set for 10 minutes before serving.

CREAMY GARLIC PRAWNS

SERVES 2

6 king prawns (jumbo shrimp),
   peeled and cleaned, tails and
   heads left on
vegetable oil, for frying
1 tablespoon butter
4 garlic cloves, crushed
2 teaspoons Cajun seasoning
250 ml (9 fl oz) double (heavy)
   cream
1 teaspoon fresh lemon juice
salt and pepper

Garnish
chopped fresh parsley
lemon wedges

Looking for the perfect recipe that is both easy to make and full of iconic FLAYVAS? Look no further than these brown butter garlic prawns! This dish is a journey for your flayvas for sure. With rich and deep buttery undertones that are enhanced by the savoury taste of garlic and Cajun seasoning, what's not to love? I serve this on a bed of creamy garlic mash (see page 103) and, woah, this dish will have you looking like a pro!

The key to achieving the perfect texture is ensuring you don't overcook the prawns because that just isn't that pleasant. This is definitely a dish that leaves you wanting more.

1   Make sure your prawns are nice and clean, then season with salt, just enough to coat them lightly.

2   Heat a large pan over high heat and add about 1–2 tablespoons of oil. Once hot, add the prawns and cook on one side until they are starting to gain some crust and have changed colour halfway through. Your prawns will go from grey to pink as they cook. Flip the prawns over and cook on the other side for another minute or so. This whole process should take no more than 2–4 minutes (depending on the size). Pop your prawns on a plate to the side.

3   In the same pan, add the butter, garlic and the Cajun seasoning. Mix over medium heat for 1 minute.

4   Now pour the cream into the pan along with the lemon juice. Bring up to a gentle simmer and cook for 3–5 minutes, or until the sauce has reduced and coats the back of a spoon easily.

5   Add the prawns back into the pan, then allow to heat through for 1 minute.

6   Finish off with a generous sprinkle of parsley, freshly cracked black pepper, a squeeze of lemon and you're done. Bam!

STICKY TAMARIND RIBS

SERVES 6

1 kg (2 lb 4 oz) baby back pork
   rib rack
½ teaspoon liquid smoke
2–3 teaspoons yellow mustard
1½ teaspoons onion powder
1½ teaspoons garlic powder
1½ teaspoons smoked paprika
1 teaspoon ground allspice
5 tablespoons butter, cut into
   small cubes
5 tablespoons light soft brown sugar
5 tablespoons honey
60 ml (4 tablespoons) Jamaican
   lager
salt and pepper
sliced spring onion (scallion),
   to garnish

Tamarind sauce
150 g (5½ oz) orange blossom or
   regular honey
50 ml (3½ tablespoons) spiced rum
60 g (2¼ oz) ketchup
1½ tablespoons tamarind
   concentrate, extract or paste
4 garlic cloves, minced
2 teaspoons grated fresh ginger
1 tablespoon reduced-sodium light
   soy sauce
¼ Scotch bonnet pepper, minced

THESE STICKY TAMARIND RIBS WILL LIGHT UP YOUR TASTE BUDS. **From the sticky, slide–off–the–bone tender meat, the first bite will have you speechless, because I know I was, and you'll be left craving more.**

The tangy tamarind in this sweet glaze is just so moreish. The meat is cooked to pure perfection, so it slides off the bone with barely any work. This dish is a perfect choice for any occasion, whether you're entertaining guests or just want to indulge in a delicious meal at home. And you know what I really love about this one? It's completely oven–friendly and foolproof. Get ready to DEVOUR these rich, mouthwatering flayvas, **which will leave you wanting more with each bite.**

1   Preheat the oven to 140°C fan (325°F/Gas mark 3).

2   Pat your ribs dry, then carefully remove the membrane from the back of the ribs. Trim any little bits around the edges that are scraggly because they'll burn anyway. Use kitchen paper for extra grip when removing the membrane. Then add the liquid smoke and mustard and rub in – this is your binder which helps your seasoning stick. Season generously with salt on both sides and a little pepper.

3   Season with the onion powder, garlic powder, smoked paprika and allspice. Some ribs have a greater surface area than others and you want the ribs to be coated in a layer of seasoning, so if it's looking a lil sparse, add more seasoning until evenly coated, but don't go too crazy on the salt as the tamarind sauce is seasoned.

4   Place the ribs on a wire rack, lined with foil (saves you cleaning), then into the oven for 2½ hours.

5   Now make a foil boat, just a little larger than your ribs, and add half the butter, sugar and honey, in the same shape as your ribs.

6   Remove the ribs from the oven and place so the top is now directly on top of the brown sugar mixture. Add the remaining butter, sugar and honey to the ribs. Carefully pour the Jamaican lager into your foil boat but not directly onto the meat. This is going to steam the ribs and get them nice and soft! Carefully seal and wrap tight, then place back into the oven for 45 minutes–1 hour, or until fork tender.

7   Now, using a stick blender or food processor, combine all the tamarind sauce ingredients. Blitz until smooth, then gently heat over medium heat until the sauce is warm.

8   Remove the ribs from the oven, open the foil and carefully drain any juices that remain into the tamarind sauce. Whack up the oven temperature to 200°C fan (425°F/Gas mark 7), carefully coat both sides of the ribs in the tamarind sauce and transfer the ribs back to the wire rack. Ensure the ribs are generously glazed with the tamarind sauce. If the ribs are super tender, carefully drain the juices, place a tray on top and flip the rack so it's top-side up again, then glaze generously with tamarind sauce.

9   Roast for 5–10 minutes, or until nice and sticky. Then allow the ribs to rest for 10–15 minutes before tucking in. It's easier to slice the ribs bone-side up for a nice slice, then garnish with spring onion.

CHIPOTLE SALMON RICE BOWL

SERVES 2–4

3 tablespoons blended chipotle in adobo sauce, or chipotle paste
2 tablespoons honey
2 tablespoons butter, melted
2 teaspoons fresh lime juice
1 teaspoon dried oregano
1 teaspoon chopped fresh coriander (cilantro)
1 teaspoon ground cumin
1 teaspoon onion powder
½ teaspoon chilli flakes
500 g (1 lb 2 oz) skinless and boneless salmon
3–4 tablespoons vegetable oil
1¼ teaspoons salt

Rice
250 g (9 oz) long-grain rice
2 tablespoons olive oil
1 tablespoon butter
2 garlic cloves, minced
1 teaspoon fresh thyme leaves
345 ml (12 fl oz) water
1½ teaspoons salt
2 bay leaves
zest of 1 lime
2 tablespoons fresh lime juice
3 tablespoons roughly chopped fresh coriander (cilantro)

To serve
Mango Avocado Salad (page 112)
black or pinto beans
Scotch Bonnet Honey Sauce (page 212)

Looking for a wholesome and satisfying meal with a Mexican influence? Try this rice bowl! The juicy salmon is cooked to perfection with just the right amount of spice to make your tongue dance a little. The coriander (cilantro) rice is perfectly seasoned and provides a delicious base for the bowl. This dish is better than takeaway and is perfect for those nights when you want a delicious and nourishing meal that won't take too long to prepare. **Guaranteed to become a new favourite for you and the ones you love!**

1   For the rice, you want to rinse it under cold water and leave it suspended in a strainer for 5–10 minutes. In a large pot or saucepan, heat the olive oil and butter over medium heat along with the rice. Sauté for 2–3 minutes, or until the rice is starting to gain colour and turn golden. Then add the garlic and thyme and stir for 1 minute, or until fragrant.

2   Pour in the water, add the salt and bay leaves, and stir everything together. You need around 2 cm (¾ inch) of water above the rice. Now bring the mixture to the boil over high heat. Once a third of the water has evaporated, reduce to a gentle simmer and cover the pot with a tight-fitting lid. Cook the rice over low heat for 10–15 minutes.

3   Once the rice is cooked, remove the pot from the heat and let it sit for 5 minutes with the lid still on; this allows your rice to steam further and get nice and fluffy.

4   Add the lime zest and juice and the chopped coriander and combine everything together.

5   For the salmon, in a small bowl, combine the chipotle, honey, melted butter, lime juice, oregano, coriander, cumin, onion powder and chilli flakes. Set aside.

6   Make sure your salmon has been sitting at room temperature for 20 minutes, then pat dry and slice into 4 cm (1½ inch) cubes. Coat in 1 tablespoon of oil and season with the salt, ensuring that each piece of salmon has a dusting of salt.

7   Heat a large non-stick or cast-iron frying pan over medium–high heat with 2–3 tablespoons of oil. Sear your salmon on all sides – this should take around 4–5 minutes – until nice and golden. Drop the heat to low–medium, pour the chipotle sauce over the salmon and coat carefully. Cook for 1 minute, then remove from the heat.

8   Serve the salmon and rice with mango avocado salad, black beans and Scotch bonnet honey sauce.

CURRIED MUTTON

SERVES 4–6

1.3 kg (3 lb) mutton, cut into 4 cm
  (1½ inch) chunks
3 tablespoons Green Seasoning
  (page 200)
2 tablespoons ketchup
4 tablespoons curry powder, plus
  2 teaspoons for burning
3 teaspoons salt
2 teaspoons all-purpose seasoning
1 teaspoon black pepper
1 teaspoon ground allspice
7 pimetno (allspice) berries, crushed
1½ tablespoons minced garlic
1½ tablespoons minced fresh ginger
1 onion, diced
2 spring onions (scallions), sliced,
  plus extra (optional) to garnish
½ Scotch bonnet pepper, deseeded
  and minced
2 tablespoons coconut oil
10 sprigs of fresh thyme
2–3 peeled potatoes, cut into 2.5 cm
  (1 inch) cubes
1 large carrot, sliced
1 whole Scotch bonnet pepper

I REALLY LOVE THIS ONE. Funnily enough I didn't eat goat growing up, which is actually the popular Jamaican dish that most people are familiar with. I never liked it until I got older and, unless you really know your stuff, a lot of butchers will sell you mutton anyway. To the untrained eye, they look the same raw. Curried mutton is something I grew up on and it was one of the first meals I mastered. I must have been around 9 or 10 years old, which feels like a long time ago now!

This recipe is really special to me because though my mum showed me how to make it, it was my granny who showed her how to make it, and my granny has always held a special place in my heart. She never got to try my cooking, but I'm certain with every fibre in my body that she would have loved my food. Not to toot my own horn, but I haven't met anyone who has tasted my cooking and not liked it. I'm running on 100% satisfaction rate, haha!

'BURN THE CURRY OR YA BELLY WILL RUN' is what my mum would always say. I can't really tell you where this came from because I've actually tested the method of not cooking off the curry powder vs cooking it off. My belly doesn't run but there's a difference in flayvas because when you cook off the curry powder, it intensifies. The truly important part is the curry powder that you use. I urge anyone that wants AUTHENTIC flayvas to use a Jamaican or Trinidadian curry powder. When it comes to this recipe, I like to use 30% bone-in meat and 70% boneless. The bones provide great flayvas and they're my favourite part to get every last ounce of meat off at the end. I don't want a curry full of bones though, because then that means less meat for me to devour. Lastly, you may be wondering why there's ketchup in this recipe? Well, it's the secret ingredient... but it's not so secret any more.

1 Alright, so the first thing you want to do is grab a large bowl, the mutton and all the remaining ingredients, except the coconut oil, thyme, potatoes, carrot and whole Scotch bonnet pepper. It really doesn't matter what order it goes in. Massage it in GOOD and allow the mutton to marinate overnight or for at least a few hours. Marinating your meat for a recipe like this is really the key to achieving the best results, so I really don't recommend skipping this step.

2 In a pot over medium heat, add the coconut oil and the 2 teaspoons of curry powder. Cook off and stir continuously for about 2 minutes, or until it's dark brown.

3   Now add the marinated meat and stir; we're not aiming to get crazy colour on this really, we're just starting the cooking process and locking in them beautiful FLAYVAS. Sauté for a few minutes until the meat is sealed, by this I mean when you see no raw parts of meat on the surface.

4   Cover with a lid and cook over low–medium heat for 15 minutes – this will allow the natural juices within the meat and veg to sweat away and start the process of creating the gravy that will accompany the meat. After 15 minutes, add enough hot water so that the meat is submerged, along with the thyme. You want the meat to be fully covered, but not too much. The water shouldn't be more than 2.5 cm (1 inch) higher than the meat. The amount of hot water you need will completely depend on the size of your pot, the cut of your meat and so on.

5   Simmer over low heat for 2 hours, or until the meat is tender but not falling apart. At this point, add the potatoes, carrot and whole Scotch bonnet pepper. Cook, covered, for a further 25–30 minutes, or until the potatoes are cooked through. Remove the Scotch bonnet pepper carefully to ensure it doesn't burst. Bring up the heat to medium and stir a little until the gravy has reached your desired consistency. A couple of minutes should do the trick.

6   Enjoy with some white coconut rice and plantain. If you're feeling extra boujee, serve with spring onion to garnish.

CRISPY CHICKEN THIGHS
& QUICK SAUCE SALAD

SERVES 2–4

6 tablespoons olive oil
2½ tablespoons balsamic vinegar
2 teaspoons honey
1 tablespoon dried oregano
2 teaspoons chilli flakes
4 skin-on, bone-in chicken thighs
1½ teaspoons all-purpose seasoning
450 g (1 lb) tomatoes (I like to use
  a mix of cherry tomatoes, vine
  tomatoes or heritage tomatoes)
1 ciabatta
4 sprigs of fresh rosemary, leaves
  picked
2 teaspoons minced garlic
2 tablespoons butter
1 shallot, diced
200 ml (7 fl oz) chicken stock
3 tablespoons harissa paste
1 tablespoon chopped fresh flat-leaf
  parsley
zest and juice of ½ lemon
6–8 romaine lettuce leaves, roughly
  chopped
6–8 fresh basil leaves, roughly
  chopped
salt and black pepper

I'M NOT REALLY A SALAD MAN, but if I'm going to have a salad it's going to consist of something a little like this. I like this salad because I can eat it any time of the year. I don't make salads so I can be on a health kick, **I MAKE SALADS TO ENJOY THEM!** I'm kinda fussy, so I don't usually enjoy a cold salad if it isn't paired with something warm, but this salad is a good mix of warm and cold, so it feels like a meal to me.

1   Preheat the oven to 200°C fan (425°F/Gas mark 7).

2   Make the salad dressing ahead of time. Combine 4 tablespoons of the olive oil, the balsamic vinegar, honey, oregano, chilli flakes and a pinch of salt and pepper. Keep at room temperature or refrigerated.

3   Pat the chicken dry and season with 1–2 teaspoons of salt on both sides, along with the all-purpose seasoning and 1 teaspoon of black pepper on the flesh side. Be sure to not get any other seasoning apart from salt on the skin. We do this as we want to render the fat and get the skin golden and crispy – any other seasoning bar salt will burn. You'll end up with a smoky kitchen and annoying fire alarm.

4   Start the chicken, skin-side down, in a cold oven-safe pan with no oil, increasing the heat to low–medium and then medium once it starts to pop and sizzle. Sear the chicken for 8–10 minutes. For the perfect sear, place a heavy pan or cooking weight on top of the chicken. The more contact the skin has with the surface of the pan, the better the sear.

5   Check the chicken every few minutes before flipping. Flip the chicken and place the pan in the oven for 10–12 minutes. (If you don't have an oven-safe pan, transfer to an ovenproof dish.) Cook until 77–82°C (171–180°F), as thighs are a fatty cut of meat and this is the optimum temperature range for a great bite. Remove the chicken from the pan and leave to rest for 5–7 minutes before tearing into chunks.

6   While the chicken cooks, slice the tomatoes into chunks or thick slices and halves. Place the tomatoes into a colander or sieve and sprinkle with ½ teaspoon of salt. Leave them for 10–15 minutes; this will season your tomatoes and draw out the moisture.

7   Tear the ciabatta into chunks and place on a baking sheet along with the remaining 2 tablespoons of olive oil and the rosemary. Bang in the oven and cook for 5–10 minutes, or until golden and crispy. Once done, add the garlic, toss and allow to cool.

8   In the chicken pan, cook the butter and shallot for 1–2 minutes until softened. Add the stock and reduce for 2 minutes over medium–high heat, then add the harissa, parsley and lemon zest and juice.

9   Put the lettuce in a bowl with the tomatoes, half the dressing, the basil and half the croutons. Toss and serve with the chicken, the rest of the croutons, the harissa sauce and the remaining salad dressing.

JUICY STICKY PRAWN KEBABS

SERVES 2–4

600 g (1 lb 5 oz) raw king prawns
  (jumbo shrimp)
2 tablespoons olive oil
2 tablespoons chipotle paste
2 teaspoons Green Seasoning
  (page 200 – optional)
2 teaspoons chopped fresh coriander
  (cilantro)
3 garlic cloves, minced
1 teaspoon medium chilli powder
½ teaspoon onion powder
½ teaspoon ground cumin
1 teaspoon salt
2 tablespoons butter, melted
juice of 1 lime
7 tablespoons honey or Hot Honey
  (page 213)
1 red bell pepper (capsicum), cut into
  2.5 cm (1 inch) pieces
1 green bell pepper (capsicum), cut
  into 2.5 cm (1 inch) pieces
1 onion, cut into 2.5 cm (1 inch)
  pieces

BBQ or oven, it doesn't matter because these prawn kebabs have MAXIMUM flavyas. **Prawns are such a great shellfish and they're pretty accessible. I like to use shelled prawns; however, that's just my preference. I can't stand having to sit there and pick away the shells when all I want to do is eat! I really love this recipe because I love BBQing, yet it's a real luxury to be able to BBQ in England. I don't think you should miss out on flavyas, so I will always try and adapt recipes to be enjoyed by everyone.**

These sticky prawn kebabs have a Mexican feel to them, especially because of the chipotle paste. Now, if you can't handle spice, I would say use half the amount listed. You'll still get all the goodness and taste, but with a little less heat. Every spice and ingredient on this list is there for a reason. I really like chopping up these prawns once cooked and having them as a topping to my tacos or in a little Mexican rice bowl sort of situation. This recipe never fails me, so I know you'll love it too.

1   Preheat the oven to 210°C fan (450°F/Gas mark 8). Soak your wooden skewers in water for 30 minutes.

2   Rinse and devein the prawns, then pat dry. In a large bowl, season the prawns with the olive oil, chipotle paste, green seasoning (if using), coriander, garlic, chilli powder, onion powder, cumin and salt. Mix and allow to marinate for 20 minutes while your skewers are soaking.

3   While the prawns marinate, combine the melted butter, lime juice and honey and pop to the side.

4   To assemble your skewers, add a red pepper piece, green pepper piece, onion piece and then a prawn, and repeat until your skewer is full. Once done, brush any remaining marinade left in the bowl over your skewers.

5   Place the skewers on a wire rack, with a little space to leave airflow for cooking, and bake in the oven for 5 minutes. Brush with the lime honey butter and then grill (broil) on high for 2 minutes to develop some char and colour.

6   To BBQ, grill over high heat for 1–2 minutes per side and brush with the lime honey butter for the last minute of cooking.

7   Serve with rice, as a starter on their own or chop up and enjoy on some tacos with my mango avocado salad (page 112).

COCONUT DAL

SERVES 4

325 g (11 oz) red lentils
1–2 tablespoons coconut oil or other
   neutral oil
1 tablespoon cumin seeds
1 teaspoon crushed cardamom seeds
1 cinnamon stick
2 bay leaves
1 large onion, diced
5 garlic cloves, minced
1 teaspoon minced fresh ginger
½ Scotch bonnet pepper, deseeded
   and minced
1 tablespoon garam masala
750 ml (26 fl oz) reduced-sodium
   vegetable stock
¾ teaspoon ground turmeric
225 g (8 oz) tinned chopped
   tomatoes
250 ml (9 fl oz) coconut milk
1 tablespoon roughly chopped fresh
   coriander (cilantro)
salt and pepper
yogurt or vegan yogurt, to serve
Chilli Oil (page 202), to serve

A ONE-POT WONDER FOR YOUR HEAD TOP! **This coconut dal is
a beautiful and easy recipe that is rich in flayvas and seasoned
with aromatic spices. This vegan dish is perfect for those who
love a balanced meal that's both healthy and flayvasome. Made
with lentils, coconut milk and a blend of fragrant spices, this
dish is easy to make and can be rustled up by anyone... it's
foolproof. The creamy texture and nutty taste of the coconut
milk complements the earthy taste of the lentils, making it a
comforting, satisfying and filling meal.**

I really do think people should cook with lentils more often,
because a little goes a long way. **Whether you're vegan or
simply looking to incorporate more plant-based meals into
your diet, this coconut dal recipe is sure to impress.**

1   Rinse the red lentils thoroughly under cold water, then leave them
    suspended in a strainer over a pot to drain off any excess water.

2   In a large pan, heat the coconut oil over medium heat. Add the cumin
    seeds and cardamom. Stir-fry for 30 seconds–1 minute. Then add
    the cinnamon stick and bay leaves. Cook for another 30 seconds,
    everything should be smelling fragrant.

3   Add the onion, garlic, ginger, Scotch bonnet pepper and garam
    masala, stir and cook for 3–5 minutes until the onions are soft
    and translucent.

4   Add the drained lentils to the pan, along with vegetable stock,
    1 teaspoon of salt and the turmeric. Stir well and bring to a simmer.
    Cook, covered, for 10 minutes over low–medium heat, or until the
    lentils have soaked up the stock.

5   Now add the tinned tomatoes and coconut milk, mix until all the
    ingredients are incorporated and cook, covered, for another
    7–10 minutes, or until the lentils are nice and tender.

6   Adjust the seasoning with salt and pepper, if needed. Remove the
    pan from heat and discard the cinnamon stick and bay leaves. Stir in
    the chopped coriander and serve with a drizzle of yogurt and chilli
    oil, and buss up shot roti (page 120).

VEGAN RASTA PASTA

SERVES 4

500 g (1 lb 2 oz) pasta (fusilli
   or penne work well)
3 mixed bell peppers (capsicums)
½ onion
4 spring onions (scallions)
3 garlic cloves
2 tablespoons olive oil
3–4 sprigs of fresh thyme
1 tablespoon tomato paste
   (concentrated purée)
1 tablespoon Wet Jerk Marinade
   (page 207)
¼ teaspoon ground turmeric
300 ml (10½ fl oz) tinned coconut
   milk, shaken
1 Scotch bonnet pepper, pierced
   a few times
2 teaspoons all-purpose seasoning
50 g (1¾ oz) vegan cheese
1 teaspoon smoked paprika
salt and pepper

THIS JAMAICAN–INSPIRED PASTA DISH is simple, fairly quick, bursting with flavours and completely vegan! **The jerk seasoning in this dish adds a beautiful kick of spice and the coconut milk comes to the rescue to balance it out and create mouthwatering island flayvas.**

This dish is often recognised by its three signature colours — red, yellow and green — hence the name Rasta pasta. There are a few variations of this recipe, but this one is the true version as it contains no meat. This is also my favourite because it doesn't matter what cooking experience you have, absolutely anyone can make this and it's a great recipe to start off with to build your confidence **if you haven't cooked much before.**

Coconut milk is used as the dairy–free option here, as it also adds a subtle sweet flavour. When I say coconut milk, I'm referring to the full–fat stuff that comes in a tin. But you don't have to use coconut milk, you can use oat cream, soya cream or any dairy–free alternative that you prefer.

1   Bring a large pot of salted water to the boil. Once the water is boiling, add the pasta and cook for 2 minutes less than the packet instructions. Drain and reserve 150 ml (5 fl oz) of the pasta water.

2   Meanwhile, roughly slice the bell peppers, thinly slice the onion and spring onions and mince the garlic. You want your pepper slices to be around 5 mm (¼ inch) thick. Save the sliced green ends of the spring onions to garnish.

3   Add the olive oil to a pan over medium heat and sauté the peppers, onion and spring onion whites along with a sprinkle of salt for 1–2 minutes, or until your onion has started to soften. Then add the garlic, thyme, tomato paste, wet jerk marinade and turmeric and continue to cook for 1–2 minutes.

4   Pour in the coconut milk, then add the pierced Scotch bonnet pepper and all-purpose seasoning. Stir and simmer for 1–2 minutes over medium heat.

5   Remove the Scotch bonnet pepper, add the vegan cheese and mix until well incorporated.

6   Finally, give your sauce a taste and adjust with salt and pepper if needed. Add the pasta to the sauce and mix. If your pasta isn't saucy enough, then simply add 3 tablespoons of pasta water at a time to loosen it up. Garnish with the spring onion greens and the paprika and it's job done!

SNA
IT UP
& SID

CK

OES

Now every meal needs beautiful sides to accompany it. This section really is about giving you the skills to take your meals to extra heights. I also love a good snack, so it was only right I shared some of my favourites with you.

LEMON PEPPER WANGZZ

SERVES 4

1 kg (2 lb 4 oz) chicken wings
2 teaspoons all-purpose seasoning
3 teaspoons Lemon Pepper
  Seasoning (page 201), plus
  1 tablespoon for the sauce
2 teaspoons smoked paprika
250 g (9 oz) plain (all-purpose) flour
185 g (6 oz) cornflour (cornstarch)
3¾ teaspoons salt
3 teaspoons black pepper
oil, for frying
150 g (5½ oz) butter
zest and juice of ½ lemon
3 teaspoons honey
1 tablespoon fresh chopped parsley

Ranch
250 g (9 oz) mayonnaise
150 g (5½ oz) buttermilk
3 tablespoons sour cream
1 tablespoon fresh chopped chives
1 tablespoon fresh chopped parsley
2 teaspoons fresh chopped dill
1 teaspoon onion powder
2 garlic cloves, grated
1 teaspoon honey
salt and pepper

LEMME GET A LEMON PEPPER ORDER PLEASEEEE! **This is a seriously underrated wing flavour, like seriously underrated. I think a lot of people underestimate the power these wings carry because they see the flavour lemon pepper and automatically think it's the safe option. I've been lucky enough to go to America a few times and let me tell you, they know how to cook wings and they go crazy for these wings. Now, me being the lovely man that I am, I've given you my very own recipe for lemon pepper seasoning in the Spice & Flavva It Up chapter (see page 201). Now, the wings are great, but you need the sauce.** If you're not using a ranch dip for your lemon pepper wings, then what are you playing at? **You don't need to order these, I've got you.**

I think the reason why these are underrated is because people assume they'll be bland or not give much when it comes to flavvas but trust me when I say sometimes less is more.

1   Ite, so boom. For the ranch it's simple: bang all the ingredients in a bowl and mix together. I like to finely grate the garlic in, as I don't really want loads of chunks of garlic in my ranch sauce. That's just me though, so do what works best for you.

2   Season your wings with the all-purpose seasoning, the 3 teaspoons of lemon pepper seasoning and the smoked paprika. Give it a good old massage and pop to the side.

3   In a medium bowl, combine the flour and cornflour with the salt and pepper. Then coat a few wings at a time in the flour mixture and shake off the excess. Place on a wire rack or lightly floured plate while you coat the rest.

4   Heat around 10–13 cm (4–5 inches) of oil in a heavy-bottomed pot or Dutch oven to 175°C (345°F) and fry the wings for 6 minutes, or until golden. Then crank up the oil to 190°C (375°F) and fry for 1–2 minutes to get the wings nice and crispy.

5   Next, melt the butter in a small pan over medium heat. Once melted, bang in the remaining 1 tablespoon of lemon pepper seasoning, the lemon zest and juice and the honey.

6   Once combined, kill the heat and stir in your parsley. Drizzle this luscious zingy sauce over your wings, toss and serve them with lashings of ranch.

CRISPY OKRA BITES

400 g (14 oz) okra
2 tablespoons vegetable oil, plus
    extra for frying
3 garlic cloves, minced
2 teaspoons grated fresh ginger
3½ tablespoons water
1 teaspoon ground turmeric
1½ teaspoons chilli powder
2 teaspoons amchar masala
2 teaspoons masala chaat
2 teaspoons ground cumin
2 teaspoons garam masala
1½ teaspoons salt
6 tablespoons chickpea flour (besan)
4 tablespoons cornflour (cornstarch)
    or rice flour
tamarind chutney, mango chutney or
    sweet chilli sauce, to serve

Crispy okra bites are rich but light, and the perfect balance of texture and taste. This recipe was inspired by a popular Indian dish that I order regularly from one of my favourite spots. This is just my take and definitely isn't authentic!

Okra, also known as lady's fingers, has been cultivated for over 3,500 years and is a staple in many cuisines. These crispy bites are seasoned to absolute perfection, providing a burst of flavvas with each bite. Now, you really want to make sure you're using the freshest okra, so it should be nice and green, crisp and have minimal blemishes. The texture of okra isn't for everyone but in this recipe it's crispy on the outside and tender on the inside, making it the perfect snack or starter. The dish is quick to prepare, making it ideal for impromptu gatherings. If you're looking for a speedy and delicious snack that is easy to make, then look no further!

1   Rinse the okra well under running water and pat it dry with a clean tea towel.

2   Trim the ends of the okra and slice them into 2 or 4 depending on the size, so slice in half horizontally and once again. Drizzle your okra with the oil and pop to the side.

3   In a large mixing bowl, add the garlic, ginger, water, turmeric, chilli powder, amchar masala, masala chaat, cumin, garam masala and salt. Mix until a paste forms.

4   Add the okra into your spice mix, really coating each piece. Ensure your okra is evenly covered in the spice mix paste. If you find that it's not evenly distributed, then simply add another tablespoon of water to loosen it up. If there's loads of excess water in the bowl, drain it before proceeding to the next step.

5   In a separate bowl, combine your chickpea flour and cornflour. Then dust this over your okra and toss in the bowl. If you find that it's a lil sticky, simply dust with more cornflour. It should be nice and evenly coated.

6   Heat a heavy-bottomed pot with around 5–7.5 cm (2–3 inches) of oil to about 185°C (365°F). Once the oil is hot, gently drop the coated okra slices into the oil, a few at a time, taking care not to overcrowd the pan. Fry the okra for 3–5 minutes until golden and crispy. Use a slotted spoon to remove the fried okra from the oil and place it on a kitchen paper-lined plate to drain any excess oil. Repeat the process with the remaining okra.

7   Serve the fried okra hot and enjoy it as a snack with tamarind chutney, mango chutney or sweet chilli sauce. You can also have it as a side dish to some dal (see page 88).

GARLIC PANKO OYSTER MUSHROOMS

SERVES 2–4

1 garlic clove
225 ml (7¾ fl oz) cold water
100 g (3½ oz) Seasoned Flour
  (page 209)
vegetable oil, for frying
150 g (5½ oz) panko breadcrumbs
3 tablespoons black sesame seeds
450 g (1 lb) oyster mushrooms,
  cleaned and trimmed

Sweet chilli mayo
200 g (7 oz) thick mayonnaise
5 tablespoons sweet chilli sauce
1 teaspoon toasted sesame oil

To garnish
gochugaru or chilli flakes
garlic powder
sliced spring onions (scallions)

If you're looking for a meat–free dish that's big on FLAYVA and texture, look no further than these mushrooms with sweet chilli mayo. Seasoned to perfection with garlic, chilli flakes and spices, these mushrooms have a rich, meaty, savoury taste that's sure to satisfy your taste buds. The panko coating gives them a crispy crunch, while the meat–like texture makes them a perfect substitute for meat in any meal. I've been screaming from the rooftops that oyster mushrooms are your best friend if you're looking for a meat substitution.

The best part? This recipe is incredibly easy and quick to make, so you can enjoy these delicious mushrooms in no time at all. Whether you're a vegetarian, a meat lover, or just looking for something new and delicious to try, these garlic panko–coated oyster mushrooms are sure to become a staple in your recipe collection.

1   In a small bowl, for the sweet chilli mayo, mix together the mayo, sweet chilli sauce and toasted sesame oil. Set aside in the refrigerator until ready to use.

2   Grate the garlic clove into the cold water, mix and then combine with the flour in a shallow dish. It should be the consistency of pancake batter.

3   In a heavy-bottomed pot or Dutch oven, heat 10 cm (4 inches) of oil to 175°C (345°F).

4   In a separate dish, mix together the panko breadcrumbs and sesame seeds; there's no need to season this as the seasoned flour has more than enough seasoning.

5   Dip each oyster mushroom in the batter, then coat with the panko breadcrumb mixture, pressing the mixture onto the mushroom to ensure it adheres well.

6   Carefully place each coated mushroom into the hot oil and fry for 2–3 minutes, or until golden brown and crispy. Then use a slotted spoon or a wire mesh strainer to remove the mushrooms from the hot oil and place them onto a kitchen paper-lined plate to drain any excess oil.

7   Sprinkle the crispy mushrooms with gochugaru or chilli flakes and garlic powder and serve immediately with the sweet chilli mayo and spring onions to garnish.

CRISPY ONION RINGS

SERVES 2–4

3 large onions
225 g (8 oz) plain (all-purpose)
 flour, plus 5 tablespoons
¾ teaspoon baking powder
2 teaspoons smoked paprika
2 teaspoons garlic powder
1½ teaspoons salt
1 teaspoon black pepper
350 ml (12 fl oz) full-fat milk
1 egg
1 tablespoon hot sauce
150 g (5½ oz) panko breadcrumbs
vegetable oil, for frying

Spicy mayo
150 g (5½ oz) mayonnaise
4 tablespoons ketchup
1½ teaspoons Worcestershire sauce
1½ teaspoons fresh lemon juice
1 garlic clove, minced or grated
1 teaspoon Dijon or American
 mustard
1 teaspoon chilli powder
1 teaspoon chipotle powder or paste
salt and pepper

I LOVE ONION RINGS, IT'S THAT SIMPLE. If I'm having a burger, I'm 100% having onion rings with it. I feel onion rings are massively underrated, but I'll be honest, if your experience of onion rings has been frozen ones, then of course you were never going to love them. You really can't beat making them yourself and they don't even take 30 minutes. These onion rings are so crispy, beautifully seasoned and paired with a quick but flayvaful spicy mayo. They're guaranteed to be a hit!

1   Combine all the spicy mayo ingredients in a bowl, whisk together and refrigerate until ready to use.

2   For the onions, cut the tops off and slice them into thick slices. Separate into rings, you'll find the centre pieces are too small for rings, so save them for a recipe that calls for onion. Onions have a thin membrane between each layer, so ensure you remove them.

3   Combine the 225 g (8 oz) flour with the baking powder, smoked paprika, garlic powder, salt and pepper. Mix and toss your onion rings in the flour and place the onion rings on a tray. Sprinkle the 5 tablespoons of flour over the onion rings and pop to the side. Keep the seasoned flour to the side as you'll need it for the next step.

4   In a separate bowl, beat the milk, egg and hot sauce until combined. Now make a well in the bowl of seasoned flour and add your egg mixture. Whisk until incorporated – don't worry, it's fine to have a few lumps.

5   Pour the panko breadcrumbs into a bowl and set up your station. It should be floured onion rings, wet batter and panko breadcrumbs.

6   Shake off any excess flour from the onion rings, submerge completely in the wet batter, drain any excess batter and then dip into the panko breadcrumbs. Only do this a few at a time otherwise it will get too messy and you run the risk of messing up the coating.

7   In a heavy-bottomed pot, heat about 7.5 cm (3 inches) of oil to 180°C (350°F) and fry the onion rings for 2–3 minutes, or until golden and crispy. Flip your onion rings every now and then and be sure to fry in batches as the oil temperature will drop if you overcrowd the pot.

8   Drain on a wire rack to catch any excess grease and season with a sprinkle of salt.

9   Serve with your spicy mayo and thank me later!

SCOTCH BONNET SPICED PORK

SERVES 2–4

600–700 g (1 lb 5 oz–1 lb 9 oz)
  pork belly, cut into thick 4 cm
  (1½ inch) strips
2 red onions
1 carrot
8 garlic cloves, crushed
4 sprigs of fresh thyme
1 teaspoon pimento (allspice) berries
1 teaspoon black peppercorns
2 teaspoons salt
1 Scotch bonnet pepper
6 dried bay leaves
vegetable oil, for frying
150 ml (5 fl oz) Rum and Ginger Beer
  BBQ Sauce (page 216)
plantain crisps (page 73), to serve

Guacamole
1 jalapeño chilli
3 large avocados
½ onion, diced
3 tablespoons chopped coriander
  (cilantro)
1 tomato, deseeded and diced
juice of 1 lime
¾ teaspoon salt
½ teaspoon ground cumin

When I developed this recipe, it was a Grubworks Jamaican take on chicharrones, a South American/Spanish fried pork belly snack made by simmering pork belly in herbs and spices and then frying it until CRISPYYYY. People always ask me what my weakness is or what I could never give up, and the answer is pork. I just couldn't do it. I've tried and failed and accepted that this cut of meat is meant for me!

My style of cooking is flavvas done well with a hint of fusion influence. I always tell people I don't just eat one type of cuisine all day, every week. I enjoy quite a few cuisines and pick up influences from my favourite foods along with the Jamaican flavvas that I've always known. That's how I've been able to develop recipes like this. Flavvas taken to the next level. I serve these with a drizzle of Scotch bonnet spiced rum and ginger BBQ sauce and authentic guacamole. My goodness, this food here? Outstanding stuff.

I like to use pork belly as it comes with the rind, then I cut it down into strips, but it's completely up to you. The results are the same and it really boils down to what you can get your hands on. I serve this with guacamole, but you can easily turn it into a little fusion bowl situation with some guac, coconut rice and mango salad. Just know that however you choose to have it, it won't disappoint.

1   So, the first thing you want to do is to add the pork belly to a large pot. Chop the onions in half, roughly chop the carrot and put it in the pot along with the garlic, thyme, pimento berries, peppercorns, salt, Scotch bonnet pepper and bay leaves.

2   Cover with enough cold water to keep the meat submerged. Bring to the boil, skim off any impurities (this will look like foam), then simmer for 1¼–1½ hours, or until the pork is tender.

3   For best results, allow the pork to cool on a wire rack and refrigerate overnight. You want to remove as much moisture as possible from the surface of the pork. If you don't have time, then wait until the pork has at least cooled to room temperature. Save the Scotch bonnet from braising, as we will use this later.

4   While the pork cools, you can make the guacamole ahead of time. I like to char my jalapeño and use a pestle and mortar to make the guacamole. It adds a really nice smoky flavva and creates a beautiful texture using a pestle and mortar. To char your jalapeño you want to do this carefully by turning it over an open flame until the skin is blackened and blistered. Then remove the stem and grind into a paste.

continued overleaf

5   Add the remaining guacamole ingredients. Mix until you reach your desired consistency. I like mine to be medium chunky. Refrigerate until ready to use.

6   In a large pan, heat enough oil to deep-fry comfortably to 180°C (350°F). Slice the pork into 5 cm (2 inch) cubes, place onto wooden or metal skewers and carefully deep-fry. **For this recipe I use a splatter screen or a lid slightly cracked open because for the first few minutes the pork will spit.** You want to fry the pork belly for 3–6 minutes until it's nice and crispy. Remember the pork is cooked, we just want it to be crispy and golden. Once done, place on kitchen paper to catch any grease.

7   In a bowl, chop and mince one-quarter of the reserved Scotch bonnet and combine with the rum and ginger beer BBQ sauce. If your sauce was refrigerated beforehand, then you want to blast it in the microwave for 30 seconds.

8   Serve the pork with the guacamole, plantain crisps and a good old drizzle of the BBQ sauce over the pork.

CREAMY GARLIC MASH

SERVES 4

150 ml (5 fl oz) double
  (heavy) cream
150 ml (5 fl oz) full-fat milk
5 sprigs of fresh thyme
5 garlic cloves, crushed
1.5 kg (3 lb 5 oz) Maris Piper
  potatoes
about 1 tablespoon salt
125 g (4½ oz) butter
pepper

Even though mashed potato is just potato it's so easy to get wrong, but so easy to make right if you know the right insider tips, which I'm going to share with you... There's nothing more disappointing than having mash that is bland, lumpy or both... YUCK. This one is a side that brings so many dishes together. It's restaurant-quality mash, without the restaurant prices or the journey.

You can use any potato to make mashed potato but I prefer a floury potato like Maris Piper or King Edward because they produce a fluffy mash. A waxier potato will produce a creamier mash, but I think it runs the risk of almost becoming gluey, so I like to avoid them. When it comes to the fats, you want to really infuse them so the flayvas are carried through in every bite. Secondly, you want to let your cooked potatoes dry a little before sieving them or using a ricer. This is because while they are still hot and wet, they'll have quite a bit of moisture and this is going to dilute the taste. I use a sieve or a ricer for mashed potatoes: yeah, it's an extra step but it's the difference between average mash and glorious mash. I know which one I'd pick each time. I really do love this recipe though because it's a great base dish to know and you can add additional ingredients like mustard, chives, cheese or even caramelised onions.

1 Alright, so the first thing you want to do is place the cream, milk, thyme and garlic in a medium pot to heat. You don't want this to boil, you just want to infuse slowly over low heat for 30 minutes.

2 While the milk infuses, peel and cut your potatoes into quarters. Make sure all the potatoes are a similar size so that they cook evenly.

3 Place the potatoes in a large pan, cover with cold water and a good sprinkle of salt. Cook over medium heat for 15–20 minutes, or until fork tender.

4 Carefully drain the potatoes in a colander and leave to steam dry for a couple of minutes, covered with a clean tea towel. While still hot, place the potatoes through a ricer and then push through a sieve using a spatula for super smooth mash.

5 Now, it's crucial you do this while the potatoes are still hot. Add the butter in cubes and mix in. Then strain the milk mixture over the potatoes, push through the garlic and beat together until nice and smooth. Season with the remaining salt and some pepper and you're done.

6 Serve as a side but try not to eat it all before it reaches the plate!

MR GRUBWORKS' COCONUT CURRIED FRIED CHICKEN

SERVES 2–4

450 g (1 lb) skinless, boneless chicken thighs
2½ tablespoons curry powder
4 garlic cloves, grated
2 teaspoons Green Seasoning (page 200)
3 teaspoons grated fresh ginger
400 ml (14 fl oz) coconut milk
1 egg
vegetable oil, for frying
1 Scotch bonnet pepper, sliced in half
2 slices of fresh ginger

Coating

225 g (8 oz) tapioca starch or cornflour (cornstarch)
125 g (4½ oz) desiccated (dried shredded) coconut
2 teaspoons salt
2 teaspoons garlic powder
2 tablespoons plain (all-purpose) flour
1 teaspoon ground ginger
1 teaspoon black pepper
1½ teaspoons dried thyme
1½ teaspoons ground allspice
½ teaspoon ground turmeric
½ teaspoon cayenne pepper

Ranch

100 g (3½ oz) thick mayonnaise
150 g (5½ oz) chilled tinned coconut milk (use the thick part of the milk)
3 tablespoons sour cream
1 tablespoon desiccated coconut
1 garlic clove, grated
1 spring onion (scallion), very thinly sliced
salt and pepper

Chilli salt

2 tablespoons flaky salt (regular, or smoked for extra flayva)
1 teaspoon cayenne pepper
½ teaspoon Kashmiri chilli powder

GET READY TO TAKE YOUR CHICKEN GAME TO THE NEXT LEVEL with this delicious fusion recipe! Inspired by Caribbean cuisine, this dish combines the crispy texture of fried chicken with the rich, tropical notes of coconut.

Now, I love Japanese food and this recipe is my Jamaican spin on Karaage chicken. If you've ever had the pleasure of enjoying that beautiful, crispy fried chicken, then you're in for a treat. If you're completely new to everything I'm saying? Don't worry, I've got you. To start, tender chicken is seasoned with a perfect blend of Caribbean spices, which add a whole lot of depth and complexity to every bite. Then, it's coated in my perfected secret coating. Well, it's not so much of a secret any more, but you get my point! It creates this moreish, nutty and crispy outer layer that will have you going back for seconds, that's if you're quick enough!

I've said it before and I'll say it again, chicken thighs are by far the best cut of chicken, after the humble wing, of course! Go into your local supermarket or butchers and see how many chicken thighs you can get compared to chicken breasts. It's a no–brainer in my opinion, but it's a preference thing, and I must admit it did take me a few years to transition over to this way of thinking.

With its perfect balance of tender meat and crunchy coating, this coconut curried fried chicken is sure to be a crowd–pleaser. And the best part? The rich flayvas of coconut and the perfectly seasoned chicken will transport your taste buds to a tropical paradise. Now, you guys know I had to buss you with a sauce recipe — these are kinda spicy because when we fry the chicken, we infuse the oil with Scotch bonnet pepper and fresh ginger. So this chicken is paired with a beautiful coconut ranch and chilli salt, and it's sexy. I can't wait for you to experience and savour this delicious and unique dish!

1   Alright, so the first thing you want to do is slice the chicken thighs into 5 cm (2 inch) pieces. Place in a bowl and season with the curry powder, garlic, green seasoning and ginger.

2   Cover with the coconut milk and mix in, making sure every piece of chicken is submerged. Marinate for a few hours or overnight in the refrigerator.

continued overleaf

3   In another bowl, mix together all the coating ingredients. Pop to the side until ready to coat.

4   **The ranch is so simple; the key is tinned coconut milk and making sure it's been chilled,** because this will enable you to use the fat that will sit at the top; it's super thick and it's great for this. Mix all your ranch ingredients in a small bowl, then season with salt and pepper to taste.

5   Remove the chicken from the marinade and place into a bowl, crack the egg into the marinated chicken and mix. Then generously coat each chicken thigh in the coating mixture, pressing the mixture into the chicken to ensure it sticks well, **NO PIECE OF CHICKEN SHALL GO UNCOVERED.** Repeat that after me. Thank you. Allow the chicken to sit for 5–10 minutes before frying – this ensures the coating sticks, but also allows for better cooking as the chicken starts to reach a warmer temperature.

6   In a heavy-bottomed pot or Dutch oven, heat at least 13 cm (5 inches) vegetable oil to 140–145°C (285–295°F). Once the oil is hot enough, carefully place a few chicken thighs into the oil and fry for 3–4 minutes, along with the slices of Scotch bonnet pepper and ginger – this will give it an extra kick! Turn occasionally. If needed, work in batches, as you don't want to overcrowd the oil.

7   Remove the chicken from the oil and place it on a wire rack to let any excess oil drain off.

8   Once all your chicken is fried, remove the Scotch bonnet and increase the temperature of the oil to 185°C (365°F). Return the chicken to the hot oil in batches and fry for another 1–2 minutes, or until the coating is crispy and golden. Remove the chicken from the oil and place it on the wire rack to let any excess oil drain off.

9   For the chilli salt, in a small dish combine the flaky salt, cayenne pepper and chilli powder. Sprinkle over the chicken.

10 Serve hot and enjoy with that cooling ranch, alone or with rice. And that's how you make Mr Grubworks' coconut curried fried chicken.

FRIED DUMPLINGS

490 g (1 lb 1 oz) plain (all-purpose)
  flour, plus extra for dusting
2 tablespoons baking powder
2 teaspoons salt
2 tablespoons white caster
  (superfine) sugar
2½ tablespoons butter
300 ml (10½ fl oz) cold water
vegetable oil, for frying

Jamaican fried dumplings are a perfect crispy, golden fried snack to accompany any hearty plate of Caribbean food. For me these bad boys are simply irresistible, when done right! Easy to make, these delicious dumplings are a staple in Jamaican and Caribbean cuisine, offering a unique experience and a taste of the region's rich history.

The process of making Jamaican fried dumplings is an easy and inexpensive one, you don't have to spend time kneading dough, you don't need a mixer, just a wooden spoon and your hands. These dumplings have a long and fascinating history, dating back to the time of slavery in Jamaica, where they became a staple. Today, they remain a cherished part of Jamaican cuisine, loved for their crispy exterior and soft pillowy centres.

I personally prefer dumplings to festivals, that's why they're in this book! I love using dumplings as a bun and making things like mini jerk chicken sliders. Now my recipe makes the PERFECT fried dumplings, but I suggest you invest in a thermometer because it's the only way you'll get this right without having to fail loads of times and waste dough! Whether you're enjoying a traditional Jamaican breakfast or serving them alongside your favourite stew or curry, these dumplings really will bring you a true taste of the Caribbean. I live in gloomy England, so anything that transports me to sunny beaches is a must!

1   In a large mixing bowl, combine the flour, baking powder, salt and sugar. Stir the dry ingredients together until evenly mixed.

2   Add the butter to the dry ingredients, then, using your hands, break up the butter so it's flaky within the dough and evenly distributed.

3   Slowly add the water to the mixture, mixing with a wooden spoon or spatula for minimal mess. Once a shaggy dough forms, use your hands to knead the dough for 2–3 minutes until smooth. Don't worry if your dough is a little sticky. It shouldn't be wet – you should still be able to handle the dough but it will have some stick to it.

4   Cover the dough with cling film (plastic wrap) and rest at room temperature for at least 2 hours, or overnight at room temperature for best results.

5   In a deep heavy-bottomed pot or Dutch oven, heat about 10 cm (4 inches) of oil to 135°C (275°F).

6   Once the dough has rested, divide into 14–16 balls. Then, using your hands, shape the pieces into little smooth balls. Make an indent with your finger in the centre of the dough, flour your ball and place it on a lightly floured plate. Repeat the process until all the dough balls are done.

7   When the oil has reached 135°C (275°F), carefully lower the dough balls into the oil, working in batches as you don't want to overcrowd the pot. Fry for 1–2 minutes – if your dough balls float straight away, your oil is way too hot!

8 Then increase the temperature of the oil to 150°C (300°F) and fry the dumplings for 5 minutes, turning regularly to ensure even cooking. Finally, whack up the oil to 175°C (345°F) and fry for 1–2 minutes until golden brown and crispy. Remove the fried dumplings from the oil with a slotted spoon and drain on kitchen paper.

9 Alternatively, to shallow-fry, heat a good old trusty pan with 3 cm (1¼ inches) of oil over low–medium heat and fry the dumplings for 2–3 minutes, turning every minute or so to ensure even cooking. Then increase the heat to medium and fry for 6 minutes, turning regularly to ensure they don't burn. It's tempting but don't heat up the oil and rush the process, as you'll end up with burnt dumplings or dumplings that are raw in the middle. Once cooked, drain on kitchen paper to catch any excess grease, and serve.

JAMAICAN CLASSIC COLESLAW

SERVES 6—8

1 medium white cabbage, half grated, half shredded
½ medium red cabbage, half grated, half shredded
2 carrots, peeled and grated
3 tablespoons finely grated onion
2 teaspoons rice wine vinegar or juice of ½ lime
3–4 tablespoons caster (superfine) sugar
1 teaspoon salt
3 tablespoons salad cream
300–400 g (10½–14 oz) thick mayonnaise
2 spring onions (scallions), thinly sliced
pepper

No Jamaican stewed, curried or jerked meal is complete without this coleslaw. Jamaican coleslaw is a family favourite that is both crunchy and sweet. **This recipe is a delicious and refreshing side dish that complements any hearty plate of Caribbean food. With just a few simple ingredients, you can make this coleslaw in no time. The combination of shredded cabbage, carrots and a sweet dressing will have everyone coming back for more. This one really reminds me of my childhood because I would have coleslaw with a side of my meal, instead of it being the other way round, haha!**

I like to grate and shred my cabbage because it provides a nice contrast in textures, **but I think coleslaw is such a personal thing. When it comes to coleslaw, I don't know a single Caribbean person who makes it the same as someone else. Whether you're serving it at a family gathering or a weeknight dinner, this Jamaican coleslaw is sure to be a winner. Serve it up with a plate of jerk chicken (see page 58), rice and peas (see page 117) and plantain.**

1 Okay, so this one? It's incredibly easy. Combine the cabbage in a bowl, along with the grated carrots, onion, rice wine vinegar, sugar and salt. Mix together, then add the salad cream, mayo and plenty of cracked pepper. The pepper amount is really down to your taste buds; I like enough to see specks of pepper in the mayo. If you want a super creamy coleslaw, use 400 g (14 oz) of mayo.

2 Adjust the seasoning if needed and finish with the thinly sliced spring onions mixed through.

3 Keep refrigerated. You'll need to mix the coleslaw before serving as the water from the veg gets drawn out and comes to the surface.

MAC N CHEEZEEE

SERVES 8–10

250 g (9 oz) smoked Cheddar
200 g (7 oz) Gouda
200 g (7 oz) Red Leicester
250 g (9 oz) mozzarella
600 g (1 lb 5 oz) macaroni
35 g (1¼ oz) butter
3 tablespoons plain (all-purpose)
  flour
500 ml (17 fl oz) double (heavy)
  cream
500 ml (17 fl oz) evaporated milk
100 ml (3½ fl oz) full-fat milk
3 tablespoons blended onion
1½ teaspoons smoked paprika
2 teaspoons black pepper
2 teaspoons garlic powder
2 teaspoons salt
chopped fresh chives, to serve

NOW LET'S TALK MAC N CHEESE! Funnily enough I didn't eat a lot of this growing up, as I didn't used to like cheese that much and was quite fussy when cheese was melted. However, fast forward to my adulthood and I learned my taste buds really do like mac n cheese...my way!

Creamy, perfectly balanced four-cheese mac n cheese. There's a few tips and tricks to get the perfect mac n cheese and there's three things you should be looking for. For me, the most important thing is flayva; it NEEDS flayvas, and cheese is tasty but you need to bring a likkle seasoning and flair to this! Secondly, the texture should be oozing and creamy, yet still a little sturdy. Lastly, cheese choices. Mozzarella is amazing for giving that cheese pull and creating a stringy texture, but it lacks taste, so you need to ensure you're picking a variety of cheeses that complement each other.

The great thing about mac n cheese is that you can really customise the flayvas and I love serving mine with perfect buttermilk honey nuggets. It makes the perfect yet simple fusion dish. THIS MAC N CHEESE RECIPE IS GUARANTEED TO BE A HIT WITH ANYONE.

1   Grate your cheeses, mix and pop to the side. Place the macaroni on to boil and cook for 2 minutes less than the packet instructions.

2   To make the roux, over medium heat, whisk the butter and flour to form a paste. Allow this to cook for 2 minutes, this will cook out the raw flour, which ensures you don't have a bitty, grainy mac n cheese!

3   Gradually add the cream and both milks (I advise mixing them together before adding them to the pot). Continuously whisk and make sure the heat is low-medium. Continue to whisk and heat up the mixture so it's hot when you add the cheese.

4   Now add the blended onion and cook for 1–2 minutes. Then add two-thirds of the cheese in two stages (remember to save a third of the cheese for coating). At this point you can kill the heat as the cheese will melt from the residual heat.

5   Then add the smoked paprika, pepper and garlic powder. Then add the salt, plus more if needed, it's really important to taste at this point. Your cheese sauce should be thick enough to coat the back of a spoon.

6   Preheat the oven to 200°C fan (425°F/Gas mark 7), then combine the cheese sauce and macaroni and transfer to an ovenproof dish. Top with the remaining cheese and sprinkle with a little more pepper.

7   Bake for 15–20 minutes or until GOLDEEEEN and brown. Finish with some chopped chives.

MANGO AVOCADO SALAD

SERVES 2—4

2 large (ripe, but slightly firm)
  mangoes, peeled and diced
3 tablespoons small diced red onion
30 g (1 oz) coriander (cilantro),
  roughly chopped
3 tablespoons fresh lime juice
1 jalapeño or medium spiced chilli,
  deseeded and diced
1 tablespoon avocado or olive oil
2 large (ripe, but firm-ish) avocados,
  diced
½ teaspoon black pepper
salt

THIS IS SUCH AN EASY AND REFRESHING RECIPE, NO COOKING NEEDED! I love a recipe that requires minimal effort, don't you? In the summer I bang this one out so much. I call it a salad but if I'm honest it's more like a salsa, especially if you finely dice everything. I finely dice the ingredients in this recipe often, especially if I'm using it for tacos. I'll keep the mango and avocado quite chunky if I'm having this as a salad with chicken breast or salmon fillets.

For me, the most important thing is making sure that your mango and avocado aren't too ripe. They should be firm but have a tiny bit of give. I like my mango pieces to be able to hold their shape in this recipe and the same goes for the avocado. I don't think there's anything I despise more than having avocado that's mushy when it's not supposed to be. Not to be dramatic, but it really hurts my soul, so please don't do that. Thanks a bunch, love ya.

1   In a bowl, toss together all the ingredients, except the avocados, pepper and salt. I like to add the avocados after mixing pretty much everything else. This just avoids it breaking down, but this is more of a personal preference thing.

2   Season with the pepper, and salt to taste – just a pinch will do. This salad does not keep too well and is meant to be enjoyed within a few hours, otherwise your avocado goes all brown and manky.

3   Enjoy on its own, as a side or with tacos (see pages 67, 154 and 158).

HOT HONEY HARISSA CARROTS

SERVES 4

2 tablespoons olive oil
3 tablespoons harissa paste
1½ teaspoons ground cumin
1 kg (2 lb 4 oz) small carrots, peeled and halved if very large
4 tablespoons Hot Honey (page 213)
salt and pepper
chopped toasted walnuts, to serve (optional)

Shawarma–style sauce (optional)
5 garlic cloves, roughly chopped
1 egg white
200 ml (7 fl oz) sunflower oil
1 tablespoon fresh lemon juice
1 teaspoon salt
1 tablespoon fresh dill
3 fresh mint leaves

HARISSA. HONEY. CARROTS. Need I say more? This recipe is something I've been doing for a minute now. I love to add a little extra flavya to my veg; it makes it so fun to eat instead of a chore! Roast dinners in the Grubworks household just aren't complete without these on the dinner table. I love to use my hot honey in this recipe (see page 213), but you can always use regular honey. Can I just say it's not just a roast dinner recipe though — you can get all fancy and serve it on a bed of shawarma–style sauce and a few drizzles of chilli sauce or dollops of harissa paste.

Now, the carrots you use are important. Those huge carrots you see at the supermarket? You don't want them for a recipe like this, simply because they are great for stews and slow cooking but lack a little sweetness. You want to use baby carrots, heritage carrots or those bunches of leafy Bugs Bunny–style carrots that will look absolutely beautiful if you keep some of the stem on. If your carrots are on the skinny side, just peel them and keep 'em whole. Pre–cut carrots are something I would stay away from too if possible. Serve these up and people will start thinking you're a professional chef!

1   Preheat the oven to 200°C fan (425°F/Gas mark 7). Get a baking tray and line it with greaseproof paper or foil and a spritz of cooking spray. This just saves you soaking and scrubbing pans later.

2   In a small bowl, mix together the olive oil, harissa paste, cumin and salt and pepper to taste.

3   Coat your carrots in the harissa paste and toss. Scatter in a single layer in the prepared baking tray and roast for 25–30 minutes. Cooking times will vary depending on the size of your carrots. Once cooked, drizzle with the hot honey, get them all coated and back into the oven for 5 more minutes.

4   To make the shawarma-style sauce, it's crucial that you remove the germ from the garlic (the green part in the centre of the clove) as this will ensure the sauce isn't bitter.

5   Next, combine all the sauce ingredients in a jug, place a stick blender into the jug and make sure it's planted firmly to the bottom. Blend and slowly work your way up, allowing a little oil to mix with the ingredients slowly. After around 10 seconds, gradually work your way up until it emulsifies. You will see this happen in front of your eyes! You'll know it's emulsified once you see no more oil and your ingredients have combined together evenly. There should be absolutely no streaks of oil. Serve right away or place into the refrigerator. It will thicken as it cools down.

6   Serve the roast carrots on a bed of shawarma-style sauce with toasted walnuts, or alongside your roast dinner.

RICE & PEAS

200 g (7 oz) dried kidney beans or
   gungo peas, or 400 g (14 oz) tin
   kidney beans or gungo peas
5 garlic cloves: 4 crushed, 1 minced
   (if using dried kidney beans) or
   2 garlic cloves (if using tinned
   kidney beans)
300 g (10½ oz) basmati or
   long-grain rice
½ medium onion, diced
6 sprigs of fresh thyme
1 teaspoon all-purpose seasoning
1 teaspoon ground allspice
5 pimento (allspice) berries, crushed
300 ml (10½ fl oz) coconut milk or
   60 g (2¼ oz) creamed coconut,
   cut into cubes
1½ teaspoons black pepper
1–2 teaspoons salt
1 tablespoon butter
1 Scotch bonnet pepper
2 spring onions (scallions):
   1 chopped, 1 whole

Jamaican rice and peas is a dish that never fails to remind me of my childhood. The aromatic flayvas and aromas always take me back to dinner cooking at my nana's on a Sunday. It is honestly a household staple and favourite that is loved by all. **Well, I haven't met a person who didn't enjoy rice and peas and if they didn't, their taste buds were awful!**

This dish is traditionally made with long-grain rice and kidney beans, which are soaked and cooked together in a flayvaful seasoned coconut milk and spice mixture, which is a combination of herbs and spices such as garlic, plenty of thyme, allspice and Scotch bonnet. You can also use gungo peas and black-eyed peas; however, you won't get that rich maroon colour that most people really know rice and peas for. You see me? I prefer it with basmati rice. **I just think it's a nicer grain that really soaks up the juices and sauces of any meat or main you serve this with.**

Once your rice is cooked, you want to fluff it and serve it alongside jerk chicken or pork, but it's also banging alone. I usually steal a small bowl from the pot before I serve it. We call that chef's privilege!

Just know if it's not fluffy, then I don't want it! **Jamaicans call fluffy rice 'shelly rice', and that's the good stuff.**

1   Thoroughly rinse your dried kidney beans a few times and soak them overnight in at least 13 cm (5 inches) of water in a large pot along with the crushed garlic.

2   Check you have enough water, at least 7.5 cm (3 inches) covering the beans to start, as when you soak the beans, you'll lose some water from rehydrating them, so top it up if needed. Place the pot on the hob and bring to the boil, then drop to a rolling boil over medium heat, partially covered, with the lid slightly ajar. Cook for 45 minutes–1 hour. Check after 30 minutes to see if you have enough water covering the beans; they should always be covered by at least 5 cm (2 inches) of water at this point.

3   You'll know the beans are cooked when you can smush them between your fingers. If using tinned kidney beans, you want to add them to a pot at this point with the 2 garlic cloves and enough water to cover them by 5 cm (2 inches).

4   Wash the rice until the water runs clear; this might seem to take a long time but you want to remove the starch! Then leave your rice suspended in a sieve to drain any excess water.

continued overleaf

5   Add the minced garlic, onion, thyme, all-purpose seasoning, allspice, crushed pimento berries, coconut milk (or creamed coconut), pepper and salt to the pot with the beans. I like to start with 1 teaspoon of salt and taste the water at this point to see if it needs more.

6   Simmer for 5 minutes, then add the rice and butter. Stir until all the ingredients are combined and the beans are evenly distributed through the rice. You want enough water to cover the rice by 2.5 cm (1 inch). You should still be able to see rice and beans – they shouldn't be so submerged that you don't see any. If you have too much liquid, simply use a mug and scoop it out, saving it just in case you need it later. It's better to start with less liquid than to have too much.

7   Bring to the boil and, once boiling and a third of the liquid has evaporated, drop in the Scotch bonnet, chopped and crushed whole spring onion, bent in half. Reduce the heat to low and steam, covered, for 20 minutes. DO NOT lift the lid before then. You hear me?

8   After 20 minutes, remove the thyme sprigs and Scotch bonnet, and set the Scotch bonnet to the side. Fluff up your rice, add the Scotch bonnet back in and place a layer of foil over the pot, along with the lid. This creates a super tight seal. If you have rice grains that look hard and uncooked, add about 3–4 tablespoons of the reserved water. Steam for another 20 minutes and you're done!

9   Serve alone or alongside some jerk chicken (see page 58). The flayvas won't disappoint!

COCONUT RICE

SERVES 4—6

400 g (14 oz) jasmine rice
1 tablespoon coconut oil
1½ teaspoons salt
2 sprigs of fresh thyme
350 ml (12 fl oz) cold water
370 ml (13 fl oz) full-fat tinned coconut milk

I COULD COOK RICE WITH MY EYES CLOSED. Growing up I had rice so much that I almost began to hate it (thanks, Mum). When I spread my wings and left the nest, I don't think I ate rice for the first 2—3 months of living alone! Now I've grown to love it again and to appreciate how well it soaks up the flavyas of curries, stewed meats and anything saucy. So here's my go-to coconut rice recipe that I love to have when I'm feeling for something a little more exciting than plain rice.

1   Alright, so the first thing you want to do is wash your rice thoroughly until the water is clear. Drain and really give the rice a good lil shake to remove the excess water.

2   In a medium pan over medium heat, add the coconut oil, rice, salt and thyme and cook for 2–3 minutes, carefully moving around to coat the rice in the oil. Try to avoid breaking up the rice grains.

3   Add the cold water and coconut milk, stir and bring to the boil over high heat. Once the liquid is boiling and has reduced by a quarter, stir and cover with a lid.

4   Drop the heat to low and cook for 15 minutes, then remove from the heat and leave to steam for another 10 minutes with the lid still on.

5   Fluff with a fork and serve!

GRATIN POTATOES

SERVES 4—6

700 ml (24 fl oz) double
  (heavy) cream
200 ml (7 fl oz) full-fat milk
1½ tablespoons minced garlic
2 tablespoons salted butter, plus
  2 teaspoons for greasing
4 teaspoons fresh thyme leaves
1 bay leaf
1 teaspoon freshly grated nutmeg,
  plus extra for sprinkling
1–2 teaspoons salt
1 teaspoon black pepper
1–1.2 kg (2 lb 4 oz–2 lb 10 oz)
  potatoes, such as Maris Piper
  or any fluffy variety
150 g (5½ oz) Gruyère, grated

THE ULTIMATE DECADENT, CREAMY, GARLICKY SIDE DISH FOR YOUR DINNERS. **Take your roast or steak game to the next level with this one. I've been lucky enough to enjoy a few trips to Paris and let me tell you, the French know how to handle a potato. This is one of those recipes where it looks daunting,** but you do NOT need to be a chef to make this.

The great thing about this recipe is that you can make it ahead of time and finish in the oven on the day. All you need to do is reserve some of the sauce to top it up the next day before doing the final bake in the oven with cheese. The dish you use is really important because you want to create layers, so there's no point using a super wide dish. You want a dish just large enough for you to be able to make at least 8 layers.

1   In a pot, add the cream, milk, garlic, 2 tablespoons of butter, 3 teaspoons of the thyme leaves, the bay leaf, nutmeg, salt and pepper. Heat over low heat for 25–30 minutes to really infuse the cream mixture.

2   Peel and slice your potatoes into pieces 3 mm (1/16 inch) thick. I like to use a mandoline but you can use a knife. Whatever works best for you!

3   Preheat the oven to 180°C fan (400°F/Gas mark 6). Brush an ovenproof dish large enough to hold 8 layers of potato (roughly 23 x 15 cm/9 x 6 inches) with a thin layer of butter, then add a layer of the sauce and a layer of potato slices and then more sauce. Continue until you run out of potatoes. If you're making this ahead of time, save 5 tablespoons of your sauce.

4   Add the remaining sauce to the top layer with a sprinkle of salt, pepper and more freshly grated nutmeg.

5   Cover with foil or baking parchment and bake for 1¼ hours. Then remove the foil cover. If you're making this ahead of time, let the potatoes cool and refrigerate at this point. Then, when you're ready to cook, all you need to do is add your reserved sauce on top before continuing on to the next step.

6   Crank up the oven to 200°C fan (425°F/Gas mark 7) and add the remaining thyme leaves and the grated Gruyère. Bake for 30–40 minutes, or until nice and golden. Allow to cool for 10 minutes before serving.

BUSS UP SHOT ROTI

Roti
480 g (1 lb 1 oz) plain (all-purpose)
  flour, plus extra for dusting
2 teaspoons baking powder
1½ teaspoons salt
2 teaspoons light soft brown sugar
400–425 ml (14–15 fl oz) warm water
2 teaspoons vegetable oil, plus extra
  for brushing
5 tablespoons coconut oil, plus extra
  for greasing
5 tablespoons butter

Chickpea curry
2–3 tablespoons coconut oil
1 onion, diced
2 spring onions (scallions), sliced
1½ tablespoons minced garlic
1 tablespoon minced fresh ginger
5 sprigs of fresh thyme, leaves
  picked
3 tablespoons curry powder
1 teaspoon all-purpose seasoning
1 tablespoon ground allspice
½ tablespoon freshly grated nutmeg
1 tablespoon smoked paprika
1 tablespoon ground cumin
3 rooster potatoes, peeled and
  chopped into bite-sized pieces
400 g (14 oz) tin chickpeas, drained
400 ml (14 fl oz) coconut milk
200 ml (7 fl oz) vegetable stock
1 Scotch bonnet pepper
salt

A FLAKY PARATHA ROTI known as buss up shot from Trinidad and Tobago. Flaky soft layers of flatbread made from only a few cheap simple ingredients. You may be wondering why it's called buss up shot? Well, it's simply because the clapping motion you do to expose the layers makes this roti resemble a torn up (buss up) t–shirt (shot).

Now, you didn't think I would leave you guys hanging and not give you a banging curry recipe to go with it?! I love chickpea curry. It's inexpensive, tastes amazing and takes just 30 minutes to make. I like to use the roti as a spoon to scoop up all the flayvas. It's the only suitable way.

1   For the roti, in a bowl, combine all the dry ingredients. Use your hand like a claw to mix the ingredients so they are evenly distributed, then gradually add the warm water to form a shaggy dough. Continue to gradually add the water until a slightly sticky dough forms. Knead for 2–3 minutes until smooth. Your dough should still be slightly sticky to handle.

2   Cover with the oil and leave to rest for 20–30 minutes. Then separate into 4–5 balls, depending on the size of your pan. If you're using a traditional tawa, then 4 balls will be more suitable. I use a 26 cm (10½ inch) cast-iron pan.

3   Mix together the coconut oil and butter and pop to the side. Roll or press a dough ball out as large as it can go on a floured surface, the bigger the better, as this is part of the layer-building process. Don't worry if it's not a perfect circle, it really doesn't matter. Then brush with the coconut oil mixture and sprinkle with flour.

4   Create one small incision from the middle to the edge with a knife or your finger. Carefully grab that piece of dough and fold it in on itself, rolling clockwise to form a cone. With the last triangle of exposed dough, fold it over the bottom to seal and pinch any other remaining dough into the seal. Then place on the floured surface and press the cone with your finger down the middle. Repeat with the remaining dough balls.

5   Allow the dough to rest for 30 minutes before rolling out on a floured surface to the size of your pan.

6   Brush the pan with coconut oil, add a roti and cook over medium-high heat, rotating clockwise for the first 30 seconds. With this roti you're not aiming for loads of colour and dark spots, this is why we constantly flip it. Brush with vegetable oil, flip after 40–45 seconds and flip once more after 20 seconds. Flip again after another 20 seconds and one last time after a final 20 seconds.

continued overleaf

7   Clap to expose the layers and store in a container with a tea towel to keep warm. Repeat with the remaining roti.

8   To make the chickpea curry, in a pan over medium heat, add the coconut oil along with the onion, spring onion (white parts), garlic and ginger. Sauté for 2–3 minutes, or until softened.

9   Add the thyme and dried seasonings and stir to form an almost paste-like consistency. If you find that it's too dry, then simply add an extra 2 tablespoons of coconut oil. Don't skip this step though, as cooking off the curry powder and spices intensifies the flavvas!

10 Then add the potatoes, get them coated in all of that goodness and cook for 3–5 minutes over medium heat, stirring regularly. Add the chickpeas.

11 Now add the coconut milk and vegetable stock and stir until incorporated. Pierce the Scotch bonnet pepper a few times, then add to the pan and simmer, covered, over low–medium heat for 20 minutes.

12 Remove the lid and add the spring onion green ends to garnish. If your curry consistency is too loose, simmer uncovered for 5 minutes, but remember as it cools it will thicken. Give it a taste and season with salt. Serve with the roti.

STUFFED PLANTAIN FLATBREADS

MAKES 8

500 g (1 lb 2 oz) plain (all-purpose) flour, plus extra for dusting
1 tablespoon instant dried yeast
2 teaspoons salt
2 teaspoons nigella seeds
1 teaspoon baking powder
½ teaspoon bicarbonate of soda (baking soda)
235 ml (8 fl oz) warm water
180 g (6 oz) plain yogurt
2–3 ripe large plantains (a few spots of brown is perfect)
½ teaspoon salt
3 tablespoons salted butter, melted
1 garlic clove, minced
2 teaspoons chopped fresh coriander (cilantro)

GET READY. I REPEAT, GET READY FOR DIS ONE! I'm not even being biased but I feel like all my food is an out-of-body experience. Think of this as a Jamaican Peshawari–style naan. If you don't know, you need to get to know. **Now, you can have these as they are or use the flatbread as a base with some chopped up leftover jerk chicken, red onions, lettuce, tomatoes, lager-spiked jerk sauce and Scotch bonnet honey sauce. Just writing this right now is even making me hungry!**

1 Alright, so the first thing you want to do is to prepare your dough. Combine the flour, yeast, salt, nigella seeds, baking powder and bicarbonate of soda in a stand mixer on low speed. I start with the paddle attachment so these ingredients can be mixed easily, then switch to a dough hook.

2 Then add the warm water and yogurt and mix on low-medium speed until the dough just starts to come together. Then change to a dough hook and mix on the same speed for about 4 minutes. It's going to look and feel a little sticky, but that's fine. It's tempting to add more flour at this point, but just trust the process.

3 Place on a very lightly floured surface and knead for 30 seconds, then form into a ball by curving your hands around the dough and shaping. Split the dough into 8 equal parts, shape into balls and leave to rise for 1 hour, or until doubled in size.

4 To mix by hand, combine all the dry ingredients in a bowl, just like the first step. Whisk the ingredients together, then add the warm water and yogurt. Using a spatula or wooden spoon, mix until the dough just comes together, then lightly flour the surface and knead for 8–10 minutes, or until smooth – it's a good arm workout, haha! Then follow the last steps and leave the dough to rise.

5 While the dough is proving, steam the plantains. Rinse them and cut into halves or thirds if they're quite large, keeping the skins on. If you have a steamer or steaming pot, steam for 10–15 minutes over high heat. **This just makes for a better texture with less moisture.** If you don't do this, follow the last steps and place them into a large pot, cover with water and boil for 12–15 minutes over high heat.

6 Strain and allow the plantains to cool slightly, peel off the skin, mash in a bowl with the salt and leave to cool.

7 Lightly flour a surface and roll out your dough balls into 13 cm (5 inch) circles. Place 2–3 tablespoons of mashed plantain in the middle on one dough circle, leaving a wide border around it. Pinch up the sides into a ball, then place seam-side down and roll lightly on the surface by cupping your hand. Place to the side and repeat the process with the remaining dough balls and plantain.

8 Heat a cast-iron frying pan or tawa over medium–high heat for 3–5 minutes, we want it nice and hot! Then roll out your dough until 5 mm (¼ inch) thick – it's fine if you can see spots of the filling.

9 Working with one piece of dough at a time, add the flatbread to the pan and cook for 30 seconds, or until the bottom starts to brown and air pockets form on the top. Then flip and cook for another 30 seconds. If you have a gas hob, place the flatbread air-bubble-side down onto the open flame, using tongs, for 10–20 seconds for some lightly charred bits.

10 Place the cooked flatbread in a pot lined with a tea towel and seal with the lid to keep warm.

11 Repeat until all the dough is cooked, then combine the melted butter, garlic and coriander in a small pot, brush each flatbread with butter and enjoy!

12 I serve this with some curry or make a loaded flatbread with seared chicken thighs, lettuce, tomatoes, onions and Scotch bonnet honey sauce (page 212).

CRISPY CURRIED SMASHED POTATOES

SERVES 2–4

1 kg (2 lb 4 oz) new potatoes or
   small red waxy potatoes
2 tablespoons flaky salt, plus extra
   for sprinkling
80 ml (2½ fl oz) vegetable oil or
   olive oil, plus 1 tablespoon for
   the sauce
250 g (9 oz) thick Greek yogurt
40 g (1½ oz) bunch of fresh
   coriander (cilantro), without
   the stems
40 g (1½ oz) fresh mint, leaves
   picked
1 garlic clove, peeled
juice of ½ lime
1 teaspoon caster (superfine) sugar
½ teaspoon salt
½ teaspoon ground cumin
2 teaspoons honey
3 tablespoons tamarind chutney
   or sauce
2 tablespoons crushed salted
   pistachios
1 tablespoon pomegranate seeds

Curry butter

3 tablespoons vegetable oil
2 teaspoons curry powder
1 teaspoon ground coriander
1 teaspoon garam masala
1 teaspoon ground cumin
2½ teaspoons hot chilli powder
½ teaspoon ground turmeric
¾ teaspoon ground ginger
¼ teaspoon ground cinnamon
130 g (4½ oz) butter, at room
   temperature
2 teaspoons flaky salt
1 teaspoon fresh lime juice
2 garlic cloves, minced

When it comes to potatoes you really can't go wrong in my opinion. If you don't like potatoes, what are you doing? **There's so many ways you can have potatoes and you're telling me you haven't found one you like?! I'm just pulling your leg, but I'm trying to emphasise just how glorious this one vegetable is. Now, these curried smashed potatoes are served on a bed of minted yogurt sauce and pistachios.** This dish is the perfect level of spice. **Crispy edges, fluffy middle and all basted in a flavaful, garlicky curry butter. The spices of the curry hum in your mouth while the minted yogurt sauce comes through to add a refreshing cooling kiss.** I ADORE this recipe.

1   So, the first thing you want to do is make the curry butter. Over medium heat, add the oil to a small pan and, once hot, add the curry powder, coriander, garam masala, cumin, chilli powder, turmeric, ginger and cinnamon. Stir regularly and allow your spices to toast for 1–2 minutes, then remove from the heat and allow to cool.

2   Once the infused oil has cooled, add it to a food processor or bowl with the butter, salt, lime juice and garlic. Your curry butter needs to be room temperature, so this means you should easily be able to poke your butter and leave an indent. Pop the butter to the side.

3   Preheat the oven to 210°C fan (450°F/Gas mark 8).

4   Wash the potatoes, then place them in a pot and cover with cold water. Add the 2 tablespoons of flaky salt and bring to the boil. Cook for 10–15 minutes, or until the potatoes are cooked through and can be pierced with a fork (NOT MUSHY). Cooking times will vary depending on the size of your potatoes, so keep an eye on them as you may need to pull out some of the smaller ones first.

5   Once cooked, drain your potatoes and allow to cool for 5 minutes before placing them on a baking tray in a single layer. Bake for 10 minutes to dry out the potatoes (this makes it easier to smash them). Take a small pan, flat-bottomed glass or a wide spatula and smash the potatoes lightly to create a flat surface on both sides. Once smashed and 1–2 cm (½–¾ inch) thick, pour over the oil and make sure it's evenly dispersed before sprinkling with flaky salt.

6   Cook in the oven for 25–30 minutes, or until golden and cwispyyyyy.

7   While the potatoes bake, prepare the cooling sauce. Bang the yogurt, coriander, mint leaves, garlic, 1 tablespoon of olive oil, the lime juice, sugar, salt, cumin and honey in a blender and blend until smooth. Remember it's a cooling sauce, so adjust with more lime, mint or yogurt if needed.

8   In the last 5 minutes of the potatoes cooking, add 5 tablespoons of the curry butter to the potatoes, carefully coat in the butter and roast for another 5 minutes.

9   Sprinkle your potatoes with a lil salt and serve on a bed of mint sauce, topped with tamarind chutney, pistachios and pomegranate.

CHILLI ROAST POTATOES

SERVES 4

1 kg (2 lb 4 oz) Maris Piper potatoes
2 litres (70 fl oz) cold vegetable
    stock
1 teaspoon salt
neutral oil or a fat like duck
    or beef, to cover the base of
    the roasting tray
3 garlic cloves
5 tablespoons Hot Honey
    (page 213)

To serve
flaky salt
1 red chilli, finely sliced
chopped fresh chives

Roast potatoes are an absolute staple in British cuisine but also loved by many British Caribbean families. Growing up my roast dinners used to be Caribbean-style. We'd have roast potatoes but we'd also have things like rice and peas and Caribbean coleslaw; trust me, the flavours made sense! You guys know I love to put my own spin on traditional recipes and that's exactly what I've done with these beautiful crispy yet sticky chilli roast potatoes with little pops of flaky salt. These are perfect for adding a likkle spice to your Sunday dinners!

Now, believe it or not, roast potatoes seem so simple yet they can go wrong. Small things like making sure your oven has been preheated is the difference between a crispy roast potato and an oily one. The type of potato you use will impact the result. Maris Piper and King Edward potatoes are the best for roasting because they are fluffy. If you use a rooster potato the results won't be the same as it's a waxier potato that holds its shape. Fluffing your potatoes is the KEY to the ultimate crispy potato. Overcrowding the pan is another common mistake I see people make. Roast potatoes should take 50 minutes—1¼ hours tops! Not heating your oil or using the wrong oil is another reason why your potatoes are taking longer. Think of it this way, preheating your oil so it's scorching hot means that when you place your potatoes in and they make that sizzle, they form a crust and that's a protective barrier forming. This stops the potatoes from soaking up the oil but also creates the crispiest edges. Lastly, pan choice, for the love of god use a roasting tray. Thank me later...

1 First, peel the potatoes and cut into quarters. We want them to all be roughly the same size so they cook evenly.

2 Place the potatoes into a large pot so they have room to cook and cover with the vegetable stock and salt. The amount of stock you need will vary depending on the size of the potatoes and the size of the pot, just ensure that the potatoes are covered.

3 Bring the potatoes to the boil and, once boiling, cook over high heat for 12–15 minutes. The potatoes should be fork tender, but not falling apart.

4 Drain the potatoes using a colander (save the stock – you can use it for soup) and let them cool for 5 minutes before giving them a little shake. This is what's going to give them that beautiful crispy texture. Place on a wire rack and leave them to dry for 15 minutes, or leave them to steam by covering them with a clean tea towel.

5 Preheat the oven to 210°C fan (450°F/gas mark 8) and add the oil to a roasting tray. Place the tray into the oven and allow it to heat up while you wait for your potatoes to dry.

6 After 15 minutes, the oil should be nice and hot. Carefully place the potatoes into the oil, coat them and roast for 50 minutes–1 hour, turning halfway through. Once you turn the potatoes halfway through, drop the heat to 180°C fan (400°F/Gas mark 6).

7 Mince the garlic, then combine it with the honey and give it a mix – this is what you're going to use to coat your roasties.

8 Toss the potatoes in the honey garlic sauce and serve with some flaky salt, fresh chilli and chives.

WOR
ON THE
STR

Now most people would say they don't have favourites when it comes to their books, well I do. This is my favourite chapter! Street food really is my thing, it's not about being fancy and pretty, it's about maximum flayvas. In this section I share a few secrets to making those street food favourites and some creations of my own.

SALT N PEPPER TOFU

SERVES 2—4

450 g (1 lb) firm tofu
3 tablespoons light soy sauce
1 teaspoon salt
1 teaspoon Chinese 5 spice
2–3 tablespoons cornflour
  (cornstarch)
about 100 ml (3½ fl oz) vegetable oil
½ red bell pepper (capsicum), cubed
½ green bell pepper (capsicum),
  cubed
½ onion, cubed
1 red or green chilli, sliced
2 garlic cloves, minced
1 spring onion (scallion), sliced
rice, to serve

Salt and pepper seasoning
1 teaspoon salt
1 teaspoon Chinese 5 spice
1 teaspoon chilli flakes
½ teaspoon caster (superfine) sugar
½ teaspoon ground ginger
¼ teaspoon white pepper

When I got the opportunity to write this book, I wanted to make sure that not a soul was left out. My vegan people, I've got you. It's funny because for some reason a lot of people forget vegan food is food...just without the meat and stuff, you know? I've never really understood the uproar! This recipe is simply just another banger that really takes tofu to the next level. The salt and pepper seasoning is the true star of the show; it's what makes you think 'How did he manage that?' I'm a magician in the kitchen that's on a mission to get everyone eating great food! I challenged myself to figure out how to get Chinese takeaway flavas at home and this recipe is a result of my testing that went right!

The thing about tofu is that, as it is, it's bland as hell. But the great thing about tofu is that it soaks up seasoning like a sponge, so it's a great substitute for meat. I like to use firm tofu. It has a lower water content so it's perfect for recipes like this. To get the perfect texture you really want to press any excess moisture out of your tofu and instead of slicing it, you want to tear it into chunks. The tearing will create scraggly edges which get nice and crispy.

1   First, combine the salt and pepper seasoning ingredients and pop to the side.

2   Using a clean cloth or tea towel, press the tofu block and remove as much of the moisture as possible. Then tear into 4 cm (1½ inch) chunks using your hands.

3   Next, season the tofu pieces in the soy sauce, salt and Chinese 5 spice. Toss and then cover in the cornflour. You want to make sure every nook and cranny is covered.

4   Heat the vegetable oil in a pan over medium heat. Once hot, add the tofu and cook for 3–4 minutes, or until golden and crispy on all sides. Stir regularly to ensure even cooking.

5   Remove the tofu from the pan and onto some kitchen paper to catch any grease. Add the bell peppers, onion and chilli over medium–high heat and toss for 1–2 minutes, or until they are just starting to soften.

6   Drop the heat to low, add the garlic and mix for 30 seconds. Then add the cooked tofu back in along with the salt and pepper seasoning. Get that tofu coated in all of them flavas.

7   Garnish with the spring onion and serve up with rice.

MAC N CHEESE BALLS

SERVES 2—4

450 g (1 lb) leftover mac n cheese
(see page 110)
100 g (3½ oz) plain (all-purpose)
flour
2 eggs
150 g (5½ oz) panko breadcrumbs
1 teaspoon salt
1 teaspoon black pepper
vegetable oil, for frying
Scotch Bonnet Honey Sauce
(page 212), to serve
chopped fresh chives, to garnish

Every time I make mac n cheese (see page 110), I look forward to turning the leftovers into mac n cheese balls, because let me tell you, the flavvas are superior! You wouldn't think a few breadcrumbs could level up something so well, but it does and it slaps.

Now when I make mac n cheese, I usually make just a little too much for my dish at home. Will I just use a larger dish? Absolutely not. Will I make less mac n cheese? Erm, no. The answer is, pop some mac n cheese to the side in a container before it's baked and make mac n cheese balls the next day! It's always the right decision in my eyes. Team it with some Scotch bonnet honey sauce and thank me later... as always. With this recipe it's crucial that your mac n cheese has set and solidified. If you try to use fresh mac n cheese it won't hold up and you'll just be left with one sloppy wet mess.

1   Portion the leftover refrigerated mac cheese into golf-ball-sized balls.

2   Then set up your coating station; you want the flour in a tray or bowl seasoned with a lil sprinkle of the salt and pepper, then crack your eggs into a separate bowl and mix. The final bowl or tray will have your panko breadcrumbs, which you want to season with the remaining salt and pepper.

3   Coat the mac n cheese balls in the flour, then in the egg and finally in the panko breadcrumbs. In a heavy-bottomed pot, heat 10 cm (4 inches) of oil to 175°C (345°F). Deep-fry the mac n cheese balls for 3–4 minutes or until golden. Be sure to turn the balls over so they cook evenly. Place on a wire rack or tray lined with kitchen paper to catch any grease.

4   Serve with some Scotch bonnet honey sauce, a few chives and dig in!

TRINI DOUBLES

SERVES 4–6

Channa
250 g (9 oz) dried chickpeas
1 teaspoon bicarbonate of soda
(baking soda)
2 teaspoons salt
2 tablespoons minced garlic
1½ tablespoons Green Seasoning
(page 200)
1 tablespoon chopped fresh
coriander (cilantro)
1 teaspoon minced Scotch
bonnet pepper
1½ teaspoons ground cumin
¼ teaspoon ground turmeric
1 teaspoon amchar masala (optional)
tamarind sauce, to serve

Bara
250 g (9 oz) plain (all-purpose) flour
1 teaspoon salt
1 teaspoon instant yeast
½ teaspoon baking powder
½ teaspoon ground turmeric
2¼ teaspoons dark soft brown sugar
200 ml (7 fl oz) warm water
neutral oil, for drizzling and frying

Cucumber chutney
pinch of salt
1 cucumber, deseeded and grated
1 tablespoon Green Seasoning
(page 200)
1 teaspoon fresh lime juice
1 teaspoon caster (superfine) sugar
1 garlic clove, grated

photographed overleaf

If you think you can just have one portion of these and call it a day, then I'm here to tell you, you're absolutely wrong. I'm just trying to let you know what to expect with this one. Believe me, I think I could eat all of these alone. You see these doubles? They're trouble!

The clue is in the name — these beautiful doubles are essentially a snack–sized sandwich, but instead of basic bread you have these warm pillowy almost flatbreads that are filled with channa, a beautifully seasoned chickpea filling. Many of the dishes you see from Trinidad are of Indian origin. There's a very similar dish in Indian cuisine called chole bhature and that's what I love about food, so many cuisines cross over and overlap.

1 I like to prepare the channa first as it can be easily reheated, so thoroughly rinse and soak the chickpeas in 1 litre (35 fl oz) water and ½ teaspoon of the bicarbonate of soda overnight.

2 After soaking, rinse the chickpeas a few times and place into a pot with 1.5–2 litres (52–70 fl oz) water, remaining ½ teaspoon of bicarbonate of soda and the salt. Bring to the boil and skim off the white foam as it cooks. Cook over medium heat for 1 hour, or until the chickpeas have softened. They are cooked when you can just squish one with your fingers.

3 Add the remaining channa ingredients and cook for 5–10 minutes, stirring often. This will help to thicken the channa. It doesn't need to be super thick, as it will thicken as it cools. Adjust the salt if needed at this point, but if you follow this method to a T, it will taste perfect already!

4 For the bara (dough), combine all the dry ingredients in a bowl and mix together. Then gradually add the warm water in four stages, kneading until combined. Your dough should still be sticky and soft; you don't want a tough dough. Cover with 2 teaspoons of oil and allow to rest for 1 hour, or until doubled in size. Then split into 12 balls and allow to rest for another 30 minutes, or until doubled in size.

5 For the chutney, sprinkle the salt over the grated cucumber and drain the excess liquid using a clean tea towel or cloth. Then add the green seasoning, lime juice, sugar and garlic and mix together.

6 With lightly greased hands, spread the dough balls on a plate until they're nice and thin. In a heavy-bottomed pot, heat around 10–13 cm (4–5 inches) of oil to 175°C (345°F). Fry the doubles for 10–15 seconds each side. They don't need long at all!

7 Place into a container with a tea towel to catch the grease and keep them covered with a lid. The steam will help to keep the bara soft.

8 Assemble by placing two doubles down, followed by a generous serving of channa, a dollop of cucumber chutney and a drizzle of tamarind sauce.

DYNAMITE PRAWNS

SERVES 2–3

150 g (5½ oz) mayonnaise (ideally Japanese Kewpie mayo)
4 tablespoons sriracha
5 tablespoons sweet chilli sauce
1 teaspoon honey
1½ teaspoons toasted sesame oil
1 teaspoon rice wine vinegar
oil, for frying
500 g (1 lb 2 oz) raw king prawns (jumbo shrimp)
1 teaspoon salt
1½ teaspoons white pepper
1 teaspoon paprika
1 teaspoon all-purpose seasoning
1 egg
150 g (5½ oz) cornflour (cornstarch)
shredded lettuce, to serve

THEY DON'T CALL THESE DYNAMITE PRAWNS FOR NO REASON, bursting with a rich umami profile, every bite is like a flayva bomb of goodness!

This one is so quick and simple; it doesn't even take 25 minutes to make. Before we start, let's get a few things out of the way. It's absolutely crucial that you're using prawns in their raw state and not cooked prawns. You'll know your prawns are raw because they should be grey, not pink! The reason I say this is that we're going to cook these, so if your prawns are already cooked, they're going to overcook, so when we get them nice and crispy, you'll end up with rubbery overcooked prawns, and we don't want that!

Now, for the best EVER dynamite sauce, you'll want to use Japanese mayo. You'll be able to find this in most large supermarkets in the international aisle, in Japanese supermarkets or you can order it on online. Although it's not the end of the world if you can't find or get hold of it, just use your favourite brand of mayo instead.

1   So first you want to make the dynamite sauce. In a bowl, combine the mayo, sriracha, sweet chilli sauce, honey, sesame oil and rice wine vinegar. Stir together until combined, then pop to the side

2   You can either shallow-fry or deep-fry your prawns. If deep-frying, in a heavy-bottomed pot, heat 10 cm (4 inches) of oil to 175°C (345°F).

3   Season the prawns with the salt, white pepper, paprika and all-purpose seasoning. Mix until evenly coated, then add the egg.

4   Add the cornflour to a separate bowl. Coat the prawns in the cornflour and toss side to side with the palm of your hand. This will get rid of any excess cornflour.

5   If shallow-frying, cook for 2 minutes per side. To deep-fry, cook for 2–3 minutes, then place on kitchen paper to catch any grease.

6   Now coat the prawns with lashings of the dynamite sauce and serve on a bed of shredded lettuce.

CHILLI LIME WINGS

SERVES 4

1 kg (2 lb 4 oz) chicken wings
1½–2 teaspoons salt
2 teaspoons black pepper
2 teaspoons all-purpose seasoning
1 tablespoon olive oil
1 tablespoon baking powder

Sauce
2 tablespoons salted butter
2 garlic cloves, minced
70 ml (4½ tablespoons) honey
100 ml (3½ fl oz) sriracha
2 tablespoons fresh lime juice
zest of 1 lime
1–2 teaspoons cayenne pepper

WINGS ARE EASILY THE MOST FLAVOURSOME PART OF THE CHICKEN **and they are massively underrated. Wings are also one of the cheaper cuts of chicken, so it's a win–win in my eyes.**

Just because these wings are baked doesn't mean they aren't going to taste great, if anything these wings are even BETTER because you don't have to feel guilty about the oil. The key to crispy wings without a drop of flour is... BAKING POWDER, **but please don't get this confused with bicarbonate of soda (baking soda), otherwise you'll be very disappointed.**

The sauce is where the real flavour comes through; honestly you wouldn't think throwing a few ingredients into a pot would create something so great, but it does. That's the great thing about all these recipes, I've walked, tripped and fallen so you guys can flourish and run!

1   Preheat an air fryer to 200°C (400°F) or the oven to 200°C fan (425°F/Gas mark 7).

2   Pat the wings dry and remove any excess moisture from the surface – this will ensure you get super crispy wings! Season with the salt, pepper, all-purpose seasoning and olive oil. Make sure you massage the seasoning into the wings to ensure they're evenly coated. Now hit your wings with your baking powder and toss.

3   Place the wings onto a wire rack or lined baking sheet, ensuring the wings aren't touching. If you overcrowd the sheet not only will you slow down the cooking process but you'll ruin the crisping process. Bake your chicken for 35–40 minutes, turning halfway. If air-frying, then simply air-fry for 25–35 minutes, turning after 15 minutes. Cooking times will vary depending on the size of your air fryer and wings. Be sure to not overcrowd the air fryer as this will slow down the cooking process.

4   Now prepare the sauce while the wings are baking. Combine the butter and garlic in a pan over medium heat and sauté for 1 minute. Then add the honey, sriracha and lime juice. Simmer over medium heat for 2–3 minutes, then finish with the lime zest and cayenne pepper. (Cayenne pepper is spicy, so if you want a spicy wing add 2 teaspoons.)

5   If you're aiming for sticky wings, brush the wings with the sauce for the last 10 minutes of cooking. If you want your wings to still be a little crispy, then toss your wings in the sauce once they're done – that's my favourite thing to do!

GARLIC PARMESAN TENDERS

SERVES 2

500 g (1 lb 2 oz) chicken tenders, or breast, sliced into strips
1 teaspoon onion powder
2 teaspoons garlic powder
1 teaspoon cayenne pepper
1 teaspoon smoked paprika
300 ml (10½ fl oz) buttermilk
200 ml (7 fl oz) ice-cold water
1 egg
200 g (7 oz) Seasoned Flour (page 209)
oil, for frying
50 g (1¾ oz) butter
5 garlic cloves, grated
2 tablespoons chopped fresh parsley
grated Parmesan, to serve

INTRODUCING THE ULTIMATE GARLIC CHICKEN TENDERS RECIPE!
These crispy, flaky and garlicky chicken tenders are moreish and addictive, with a serious crunch and a beautiful coating that's dusted with Parmesan.

The secret to making the chicken moist is the wet brine of buttermilk. The acidity helps to break down the meat and make it tender. However, there is such a thing as marinating for too long. If you leave the chicken in the buttermilk for too long, the meat breaks down and starts to turn into mush. A big no-no.

My signature coating really elevates this recipe, along with the garlic butter and Parmesan. **Whether you're frying up a batch for a weekend treat or making them to impress your family and friends, you'll be the favourite of your circle for a while.**

1 First, season the tenders with half the onion powder, the garlic powder, cayenne pepper and smoked paprika, mix and then cover with the buttermilk. Make sure they're all submerged and allow to marinate for at least 4 hours or overnight.

2 Remove the tenders from the buttermilk, trying to remove as much buttermilk as possible. Pat the tenders dry with kitchen paper, removing as much moisture from the surface as possible.

3 Add the cold water and egg to the leftover buttermilk. Give it a mix and pop to the side. Set up a bowl with the seasoned flour, along with a tray and a wire rack.

4 Dip your fingers in the buttermilk mixture and distribute little droplets throughout the seasoned flour. Shake the bowl side to side and repeat this 2–3 times. This will form flakes in the batter, which will create the perfect crust on your chicken.

5 Now coat the tenders in the seasoned flour, shake off any excess flour, then coat in the wet buttermilk, shake off the excess and lastly coat in the seasoned flour once more. Toss your chicken side to side like a hot potato to create those perfect flakes. Leave for 5 minutes on the wire rack before frying.

6 In a heavy-bottomed pot or Dutch oven, heat 13 cm (5 inches) of oil to 140–145°C (285–295°F). Fry the tenders for 3–4 minutes, moving around carefully after a minute. Remove from the oil. You may need to work in batches – just make sure you don't overcrowd the oil.

7 Once all the chicken is fried, whack up the temperature to 185–190°C (365–375°F) and fry the chicken for 1–2 minutes until crispy. Place on a wire rack and allow to cool for a few minutes.

8 Over medium heat, combine the butter, garlic and remaining onion powder. Mix until combined or until smelling fragrant. Kill the heat, add the parsley and it's done.

9 Drizzle your tenders with the garlic butter and finish with a generous coating of Parmesan. Enjoy!

SCOTCH BONNET CALAMARI

SERVES 2–4

500 g (1 lb 2 oz) squid
150 g (5½ oz) cornflour (cornstarch)
300 ml (10½ fl oz) buttermilk
200 g (7 oz) plain (all-purpose) flour
2 tablespoons garlic powder
2 tablespoons onion powder
1 tablespoon paprika
2½ teaspoons salt
2 teaspoons black pepper
1 teaspoon dried thyme
vegetable oil, for frying

Garlic mayo
225 g (8 oz) thick mayonnaise
3 garlic cloves, grated or minced
2 teaspoons fresh lemon juice
1 teaspoon Dijon mustard
salt

Chilli salt
2 tablespoons flaky salt (regular,
   or smoked for extra flayvas)
½ teaspoon cayenne pepper
1 teaspoon Kashmiri chilli powder

To serve
chopped fresh parsley
sliced red chilli
lemon wedges

Looking for a restaurant–quality seafood dish that is quick, surprisingly easy and bursting with real FLAYVA? Look no further than this Scotch bonnet calamari with a garlic lemon mayo sauce. Now I don't know about you lot, but when I see calamari on the menu, I'm getting that! Saying that, I'm disappointed more times than I'm not. But with this recipe? It's perfect. With its crispy, spicy twist, this addictive calamari takes your taste buds on a wild journey that you won't forget. The combination of Scotch bonnet pepper and calamari provides a banging explosion of spice and flayvas that will leave you wanting more. It's almost like a Caribbean twist on calamari.

I make a Scotch bonnet salt that you hit the calamari with while it's crispy and piping hot. Yeah, just talking about it now is reminding me why I love this so much. The joys of being a chef and being able to elevate your favourite dishes. The Scotch bonnet salt is so incredibly easy to make and if you're a lover of spice, this recipe is really going to be up your street. Get ready to enjoy a crispy, spicy and seafood–filled experience. Grab your apron and get ready to impress...

1   Start by making your garlic mayo – it's pretty simple really. Add the mayonnaise to a bowl, add the garlic, lemon juice, Dijon mustard and stir. Add salt to taste and pop to the side.

2   For the chilli salt, in a pestle and mortar, combine the flaky salt, cayenne and chilli powder. Pop to the side until ready to use.

3   Clean the squid under cold running water and remove the skin. Then cut just below the eyes, keeping the tentacles, as we don't waste these beauties. Pull the quill, a clear plastic-like structure, from the inside. Rinse again under running water and pat dry.

4   Cut the body into rings, dust with 1½ tablespoons of the cornflour, then cover all the squid with the buttermilk and marinate while you prepare the coating. In a bowl, combine the flour, remaining cornflour, garlic powder, onion powder, paprika, salt, pepper and thyme.

5   In a deep frying pan, heat about 7.5–10 cm (3–4 inches) of oil to 180–190°C (350–375°F). Take the squid rings and tentacles out of the buttermilk mixture, shake off the excess buttermilk and dredge them in the flour mix until fully coated. Be sure to work in batches, you don't want to overcrowd the flour.

6   Carefully place the coated squid in the hot oil and fry for about 2 minutes, or until golden and crispy. Squid doesn't take long – that's why we fry it hot and fast because chewy squid is a big no.

7   Using a slotted spoon, remove the squid from the oil and place on kitchen paper to drain any excess oil. Immediately sprinkle the chilli salt over the squid and garnish with parsley and red chilli and a few wedges of lemon. Dunk in your sauce and get lost in these flayvas!

COCONUT PRAWNS

SERVES 2

650 g (1 lb 7 oz) large raw king
    prawns (jumbo shrimp)
4 teaspoons Cajun seasoning
    (store-bought or see recipe below)
1 teaspoon ground ginger
125 g (4½ oz) plain (all-purpose)
    flour
150 ml (5 fl oz) cold water
150 ml (5 fl oz) coconut milk
1 egg
100 g (3½ oz) unsweetened
    desiccated (dried shredded)
    coconut
vegetable oil, for frying
salt

Quick Cajun seasoning mix
2 tablespoons smoked paprika
1 tablespoon salt
1 tablespoon garlic powder
1 tablespoon onion powder
1½ teaspoons black pepper
½ tablespoon dried thyme
½ tablespoon cayenne pepper
½ tablespoon dried oregano

Burnt chilli mayo
1 red chilli
200 g (7 oz) mayonnaise
zest of ½ lime, plus 1 teaspoon juice
2 teaspoons honey

These prawns? THESE PRAWNS? There's not many things I wouldn't do for a plate of prawns, my gardd. **The coconut really is the star of the show here. For me, the coconut brings that coconut taste, but it's not too in your face, you know? You can't really go wrong with prawns, just don't overcook them and you're good! I don't think there's anything that upsets me more than overcooked rubbery prawns — yuck.**

It's crucial with this recipe that you use raw prawns. Raw prawns are grey, not pink. They can be fresh or frozen (but thawed), they just can't be cooked prawns. Think of it this way, if you're going to coat and cook a prawn that's already cooked, any more heat you add will overcook it and that's a big no–no. Another crucial step is using good coconut milk. I'm not talking about the stuff in a carton. I'm talking about proper tinned stuff, that's the good stuff.

You can buy Cajun seasoning, but a lot of people don't know it's really, really easy to make your own. I've included a quick Cajun seasoning mix too because you know I'll always go above and beyond for you!

1   First, make the Cajun seasoning mix by combining all the ingredients in a bowl. If you're using a store-bought one (totally not judging you), then skip this step.

2   Rinse the prawns, carefully butterfly them and remove the digestive tract. Keep the tails on if they do have them as it just makes it easier when you start coating them.

3   Season the prawns with 2 teaspoons of the Cajun seasoning, the ginger and ½ teaspoon of salt and pop to the side while you make your batter.

4   In a separate bowl, combine the flour with another 2 teaspoons of Cajun seasoning and whisk. Then add the cold water, coconut milk and egg. Whisk away until smooth; don't worry if there's a few tiny lumps. Now seasoning is key, so add a sprinkle of salt to the desiccated coconut and mix together.

5   In a heavy-bottomed pot, Dutch oven or deep-fat fryer, heat 5–7.5 cm (2–3 inches) of oil to 175°C (345°F). Coat the prawns in the batter, using the tail to grip the prawns. Let the excess drip off and then coat in the coconut mixture. Only do a few prawns at a time, then allow your coating to stick for 5 minutes.

6   While your prawns sit, prepare the burnt chilli mayo. Char your chilli over an open flame until the skin has started to blacken and blister. Remove the stem and mince until a paste has formed. Combine with your mayo, lime zest and juice and honey.

7   Lastly, fry the prawns for 3 minutes, or until golden and crispy! Place them on kitchen paper or a wire rack to drain any excess grease.

8   Enjoy with the burnt chilli mayo!

SWEET & SOUR CHICKEN

SERVES 2–4

500 g (1 lb 2 oz) skinless, boneless chicken thighs or breasts
2 tablespoons reduced-sodium light soy sauce
1 egg
2 garlic cloves, minced
65 g (2¼ oz) plain (all-purpose) flour, plus 2 tablespoons
65 g (2¼ oz) cornflour (cornstarch)
1 teaspoon onion powder
1 teaspoon garlic powder
1 teaspoon baking powder
vegetable oil, for frying
½ onion, cubed
½ red bell pepper (capsicum), chopped into bite-sized cubes
½ green bell pepper (capsicum), chopped into bite-sized cubes
200 g (7 oz) tinned pineapple, cubed
1 teaspoon sesame seeds
salt and white pepper
rice, to serve

Sweet and sour sauce
100 ml (3½ fl oz) reduced-sodium chicken stock
75 ml (3½ tablespoons) pineapple juice, reserved from the tin
6 tablespoons ketchup
4 tablespoons caster (superfine) sugar
3 tablespoons white vinegar
1 tablespoon oyster sauce
2 garlic cloves, minced
1 tablespoon cornflour (cornstarch)

LISTEN GOOD AND LISTEN NOW when I tell you that you don't need to order this from your favourite takeaway any more! **I mean you still can, but I'm dropping the secrets to the game guys because I feel like everyone should have a few of their favourite takeaway orders in their recipe arsenal. If someone made this for me, I'd be impressed, you know? The flayvas are just so good that a lot of the time whenever I try sweet and sour chicken that isn't my own I'm kind of disappointed. That really tells you everything you need to know about how certi this recipe is.**

You can use chicken thighs or breasts. It genuinely is a preference thing. **Thighs are cheaper and more forgiving but a lot of people prefer white meat for these sorts of recipes. If you're genuinely trying to achieve authentic takeaway flavours, then this is the one for you. Like I said from the start, I've got you!**

1   Slice the chicken into rough 5 cm (2 inch) pieces, then place into a bowl and season with the soy sauce, ¾ teaspoon of salt, ½ teaspoon of white pepper, the egg, garlic and the 2 tablespoons of flour. Mix and pop to the side to marinate for 15–20 minutes while you prepare the chicken coating and sauce.

2   In a separate bowl, combine the 65 g (2¼ oz) flour, the cornflour, ½ tablespoon of salt, 1 teaspoon of white pepper, the onion powder, garlic powder and baking powder. Whisk and pop to the side.

3   For the sauce, bang the chicken stock, pineapple juice, ketchup, sugar, vinegar, oyster sauce, garlic and cornflour in a bowl, give it a good mix and pop to the side.

4   In a wok or heavy-bottomed pan, heat around 5–7.5 cm (2–3 inches) of oil to 165°C (330°F). Give the chicken a quick mix again, shake off any excess marinade and carefully coat a few pieces of chicken at a time in the flour mixture. Make sure every part of the chicken is coated in that flour!

5   Fry the chicken for 4 minutes, or until golden, moving every now and then to ensure it doesn't burn. Remove the chicken from the oil, crank it up to 175°C (345°F) and fry the chicken for 1–2 minutes until cwispyyyyy.

6   Discard the oil, keeping 1 tablespoon in the wok or pan. Sauté the onion and bell peppers over medium–high heat for 1–2 minutes, or until they've just started to soften. Then toss in the pineapple and cook for a further minute before adding the sweet and sour sauce. Allow this to thicken over medium heat for 30 seconds–1 minute.

7   Add the chicken back into the mix and toss in that beautiful sauce. Garnish with the sesame seeds and serve with rice.

OXTAIL GYOZAS

SERVES 2–4

1 Chinese napa cabbage
1 teaspoon salt
450 g (1 lb) leftover oxtail, shredded
  and removed from the bone
2 spring onions (scallions),
  thinly sliced
2 teaspoons sesame oil
1 teaspoon chopped fresh coriander
  (cilantro)
180–250 g (6–9 oz) frozen gyoza
  wrappers, defrosted
1–2 tablespoons vegetable oil

Gyoza salsa

3 tablespoons chopped coriander
  (cilantro)
1½ spring onions (scallions),
  thinly sliced
2 teaspoons grated garlic
1 teaspoon grated fresh ginger
5 tablespoons light soy sauce
5 tablespoons rice wine vinegar
2 tablespoons crispy chilli oil
1 tablespoon toasted sesame oil
2 teaspoons caster (superfine) sugar
2 teaspoons toasted sesame seeds

OXTAIL GYOZAS... ARE YOU LISTENING?! Is this a dream? No,
I did that. A fusion of my two favourite cuisines. This dish
combines the best of both worlds – Japanese and Jamaican
cuisine. These beautiful, succulent and addictive dumplings
are filled with tender, slow-braised oxtail meat and wrapped
in a crispy gyoza skin. The gyoza salsa with chilli oil adds a
spicy kick to the already flayvaful dish. And yes, before you
ask, there's a recipe for chilli oil, just flick a few pages to
page 202. I like to use frozen gyoza wrappers because they're
proper, cheap and convenient. I wanted to include a dough
recipe, but when I originally made this, it was quick and fun,
so it had to stay that way.

Now before you start moaning and whining and saying who has
leftover oxtail, I DO, OKAY. This recipe was a happy accident
that I wanted to share. It's definitely worth making oxtail for this
alone! This is a recipe that I get to enjoy a few times a year and
it's definitely a treat. Gyozas are enjoyed all over the world and
I don't meet or hear many people saying they don't like them.
Steamed or fried, it nuh matter! This fusion recipe takes you on
a flayva journey like no other. Indulge in these delicious gyozas
for a unique out-of-body culinary experience by yours truly.
You might even feel like I made this one for you personally.

1   Chop the cabbage into small pieces. Place in a bowl along with the
    salt and mix well. Allow it to sit for 30 minutes at room temperature
    to draw out the moisture. Then, using a muslin cloth or clean tea
    towel, squeeze out the excess water from the cabbage.

2   In a separate bowl, mix the oxtail, spring onions, 1 teaspoon of the
    sesame oil, the coriander and the squeezed cabbage. I can't lie, this
    is a mix-by-hand job as the oxtail will be quite gelatinous since it's
    already been cooked down and refrigerated as leftovers.

3   To assemble the gyoza, take one gyoza wrapper and place a small
    spoonful of the oxtail filling in the centre. Dip your finger in a bowl
    of water and run it along the edge of the wrapper to moisten it.

4   Fold the wrapper in half, pinch the middle and create folds on each
    side to seal – don't worry, this is quite fiddly and takes A LOT of
    practice to perfect. As long as they're sealed, that's the important
    thing. Repeat with the remaining gyoza wrappers and filling.

5   Heat a non-stick frying pan over medium–high heat. Once hot,
    add 1–2 tablespoons of vegetable oil. Place the gyozas in the pan,
    ensuring they do not touch each other, and cook until the bottom
    of the gyozas are golden brown.

6   Add 60 ml (4 tablespoons) water to the pan and cover immediately
    with a lid. Cook for 3 minutes, or until the water has evaporated and
    the gyoza wrappers are cooked through.

7   Remove the lid, add the remaining teaspoon of sesame oil and cook
    until the gyozas are crisp and golden brown on the bottom.

8   To make the gyoza salsa, mix all the ingredients together in a bowl.
    Serve the salsa as a dip or use it to garnish, along with extra chilli oil.
    The flayvas? PHENOMENAL.

HOT HONEY CHICKEN NUGGETS

SERVES 4

1 kg (2 lb 4 oz) chicken breasts or
  skinless, boneless thighs
2 teaspoons onion powder
2 teaspoons garlic powder
2 teaspoons cayenne pepper
2 teaspoons smoked paprika
2 teaspoons black pepper
600 ml (21 fl oz) buttermilk
350 g (12 oz) Seasoned Flour
  (page 209)
vegetable oil, for frying
Hot Honey (page 213)

BANGING AND BEAUTIFUL IS THE ONLY WAY TO DESCRIBE THESE NUGGETS — beautifully seasoned, beautifully moist, covered in a beautiful coating and lashings of Hot Honey (see page 213). You absolutely can't go wrong with these. They are way better than the processed stuff and they're really easy to make.

The key to the perfect flaky nuggets is the technique and coating — once you've got that in the bag, the rest is simple. I've played around with this recipe a lot, tweaking measurements and deciding between cornflour or just a flour coating. When it comes to textures and crunches, you guys know that's my bag, however, I do believe there is such a thing as too crunchy when it comes to fried chicken. Now some people will say don't use flour, but if we're talking chicken that's not being coated in a sauce, then you absolutely want some flour to balance out the dryness of using any form of starch. I swear by my seasoned flour recipe.

Now, you can use breast or thigh meat; thighs are way juicier and definitely more forgiving if you don't have time to marinate your chicken. I prefer breast for nuggets, but in all honesty it's personal preference. You can shallow-fry these or deep-fry them, but of course the best results are from deep-frying as they'll cook quicker and more evenly. Remember you don't need a deep-fryer to deep-fry. A deep heavy-bottomed pot can be used to deep-fry too.

I'm telling you every bite will be an experience you don't want to end.

1   The first thing you want to do is slice the chicken into roughly 3 cm (1¼ inch) pieces. The size is really up to you, but obviously the smaller the chicken, the quicker it will cook.

2   Place the chicken in a bowl and season with the onion powder, garlic powder, cayenne pepper, smoked paprika and black pepper. Give it a good mix – don't be shy!

3   Cover with the buttermilk and allow to marinate for at least 5 hours (you can also leave this overnight). You don't have to marinate for hours; if you want you can skip straight to the coating process.

4   Now shake off any excess buttermilk from your chicken into the seasoned flour, this is what will help to create layers and texture in your coating. Shake around your flour bowl so the droplets of buttermilk get lost in the flour. Then place the chicken into the seasoned flour. Be sure to do no more than three pieces of chicken at a time, as we don't want to overcrowd the flour.

5   Give your pieces of chicken one tight squeeze and then submerge and cover with flour. You want to toss the chicken between both hands, side to side for 10 seconds (imagine it's hot!). This is going to create the flakes and layers. Repeat the process with all the chicken, then place onto a tray and allow to sit for 5 minutes before frying.

6   In a heavy-bottomed pot, heat around 10–13 cm (4–5 inches) of oil to 175°C (345°F), then carefully place your nuggets into the oil. After a minute, move them around. You will need to fry in batches, depending on the size of your pot. The chicken should take 4–5 minutes to cook, or use a temperature probe and remove it once it reaches an internal temperature of 74°C (165°F). I like to fry my chicken at 140°C (285°F) for 3 minutes, remove the chicken and place it on a wire rack, then crank up the oil to 175°C (345°F) and fry for 1–2 minutes until crispy.

7   Place on a wire rack or tray lined with kitchen paper to catch any grease. Once done, heavily drizzle with hot honey and you're done!

JAMAICAN BEEF PATTIES

MAKES 6–8 PATTIES

1 teaspoon garlic powder
1 teaspoon onion powder
1 teaspoon ground ginger
1 teaspoon all-purpose seasoning
1 teaspoon black pepper
1 teaspoon salt
500 g (1 lb 2 oz) beef mince
   (15–20% fat)
2 teaspoons vegetable oil
1 small onion, finely diced
1 carrot, peeled and finely diced
2 garlic cloves, minced
2 spring onions (scallions),
   thinly sliced
½–1 Scotch bonnet pepper (with
   seeds for spice)
2 tablespoons fresh thyme leaves
1 teaspoon tomato paste
   (concentrated purée)
3 tablespoons dark soy sauce
55 g (2 oz) ketchup
2 teaspoons browning
150 ml (5 fl oz) hot water
5 tablespoons fine white or panko
   breadcrumbs

Dough

480 g (1 lb 1 oz) plain (all-purpose)
   flour, plus extra for dusting
1 teaspoon baking powder
2 teaspoons cornflour (cornstarch)
1 teaspoon curry powder
1 teaspoon ground turmeric
2 teaspoons caster (superfine) sugar
1½ teaspoons salt
200 g (7 oz) beef dripping or suet,
   cut into small cubes and frozen
150 ml (5 fl oz) ice-cold water
100 ml (3½ fl oz) ice-cold buttermilk
2 teaspoons white vinegar
2 tablespoons yellow food colouring
   powder (optional, but it really gets
   that authentic colour!)
20 g (¾ oz) butter, cut into cubes
   and frozen
1 egg, beaten

IT TOOK ME A LONG, LONG TIME TO DECIDE if I would include this recipe because it's taken me 7 years to perfect. My longest ongoing project! **Jamaican beef patties are a delicious and popular snack that bring back childhood memories for many people, especially me.**

These beautiful patties are filled with juicy, perfectly seasoned beef and wrapped in a flaky pastry crust that is sure to satisfy any craving. Don't get it twisted though, I've had some awful patties in my short 25 years of life. The crust is so, so important. If you don't have crumbs on your mouth or on you when you're eating a patty, then it just simply isn't 10/10. **Don't argue with me, I don't make the rules!**

The history of patties can be traced back to Jamaica, where they were originally sold as street food. Today, these addictive treats are enjoyed all over the world. To make the best Jamaican beef patties, you start by preparing the rich, spicy, beef filling with a blend of herbs and spices that are commonly used in Jamaican cuisine. The crust should be flaky, heavy on the FLAKY and if it's not that famous yellow colour, I don't want it. **For the best results, you want to ideally be using a block of beef dripping. Not the liquid stuff, that won't work for this recipe.**

Whether you're enjoying these patties for a trip down memory lane or trying them for the first time, they are sure to become an all-time favourite. I really hope you enjoy this recipe because my heart and soul went into this one. It's been my baby for the longest time and I was finally persuaded to share the perfected version with you.

1   Okay, so it's actually easier to start by preparing the filling because you'll want this to cool down before filling your patties.

2   In a small bowl, mix the garlic and onion powders, ginger, all-purpose seasoning, pepper and salt. Season the beef with half of this seasoning and pop to the side.

3   Over medium heat, add the oil to a non-stick pan and sauté the onion and carrot for 2–3 minutes, or until softened. Then add the garlic, spring onions, Scotch bonnet and thyme. Cook for another 1–2 minutes, or until fragrant. Then add the tomato paste, soy sauce and ketchup. Let this cook down, stirring regularly for 2 minutes.

continued overleaf

4 Now add the beef, then use the back of a spoon to really break it down. **It's really important that you break it down because you don't want big chunks of beef mince.** Once your meat is broken down into a crumb-like consistency, add the browning and half the hot water. Give it a good mix and cook, covered, over low heat for 10–15 minutes.

5 Then add the breadcrumbs, remaining seasoning mixture and remaining hot water and mix well. Cook for a further 5 minutes, or until the mixture is nice and moist, yet soft. The breadcrumbs are crucial in creating the right consistency, as they soak up the moisture. Once cooked, double check for seasoning and spice, and adjust if needed.

6 **At this point your filling is done!** Allow to cool while you make the dough.

7 In a bowl, combine the flour, baking powder, cornflour, curry powder, turmeric, sugar and salt. Mix with a whisk until the ingredients are evenly distributed.

8 Now add the beef dripping pieces, straight from the freezer, and use a spoon or your hands to quickly toss and get coated in the flour.

9 In a jug, combine the ice-cold water, buttermilk, vinegar and yellow food colouring powder (if using). Notice how everything is cold, this is the key to making the perfect pastry. It keeps the fats cold, so once they go into the oven they'll melt between the layers, which creates pockets in the pastry and results in a flaky crust.

10 Pour the wet mixture into the flour bowl and use a wooden spoon to mix. It will be quite hard to mix, but you don't want to use your hands at this point. Once the ingredients have come together, tip onto a lightly floured surface.

11 Knead for a minute or until a dough has formed. You want the ingredients to just come together, lumps of beef dripping is what you want. The dough should be full of it! Wrap in cling film (plastic wrap) and transfer to the refrigerator to chill for 30 minutes.

12 Flour the work surface and roll out the dough to 1 cm (½ inch) thick, keeping it rectangular. Then fold the bottom to the middle and the top to the middle (like you're folding a letter).

13 Turn over (so the seam side should be down), then roll out again and repeat once more. What we're doing is almost like a puff pastry technique, which creates layers. Repeat twice more. Refrigerate for 20 minutes.

14 Roll out the dough once more, repeat the folding process twice more and scatter the frozen butter cubes across the dough. Fold like a letter again and roll once more. Now after rolling this time, you want to fold it up again and roll it to 3 cm (1¼ inch) thick, then split into 6–8 equal sections.

15 Preheat the oven to 180°C fan (400°F/Gas mark 6).

16 Working with one section at a time, on a floured surface, roll out the dough to 5 mm (¼ inch) thick. Now, you can keep the dough as a rectangle, which means you won't have to cut the edges and roll any dough, or you can place the dough onto a bowl to create a perfect round, which makes the traditional half-moon patty shape. **Opt for whatever works best for you.**

17 Scoop 4–5 tablespoons of the cooled filling into the centre of the dough, leaving space round the edges to seal. Then brush the sides with beaten egg with your finger or pastry brush and fold the dough over, pressing gently to push the air out and to seal. Press the edges of the patty using a fork dipped in flour. Trim the edges using a pizza cutter or knife. Carefully dust your patties with more flour.

18 Add the patties to an oven tray lined with baking parchment and dusted with plenty of flour or make sure you're using a trusted tray that doesn't cause sticking. **I like to use a dark tray as this creates a nice golden bottom.**

19 Bake for 25–30 minutes, or until golden, crispy and flaky. Allow to cool for 5 minutes before enjoying!

BIRRIA TACOS

SERVES 4—6

vegetable oil, for frying
2 onions: 1 halved, 1 finely diced
3 tomatoes
8 garlic cloves
2 tablespoons dried oregano,
   preferably Mexican
2 teaspoons fresh thyme leaves
4 cloves
1 teaspoon black peppercorns
1 carrot, peeled and halved
1.3 kg (3 lb) bone-in beef short ribs,
   trimmed
300 g (10½ oz) bone-in beef shank
1–2 teaspoons salt
2 teaspoons ground cumin
1 teaspoon black pepper
800 ml–1 litre (28–35 fl oz) beef
   stock
2 tablespoons apple cider vinegar
¾ teaspoon ground ginger
16–18 small corn tortillas
500 g (1 lb 2 oz) mozzarella, grated
1 bunch of fresh coriander (cilantro),
   roughly chopped
3 limes, sliced into wedges

Chillies
2 guajillo
3 de arbol
2 ancho
1 chipotle
1 pasilla
1 mulato

A big shout out to my guy Pedro and his wonderful grandmother who took the time to educate me on the history of birria. **I think it's really important when you embrace a cuisine that's not native to you that you educate yourself on the history of said foods.** Birria is a slow–cooked stew traditionally made with goat meat and a flayvaful blend of spices, chillies and herbs, and has been a beloved dish in Mexico for generations.

The history of birria can be traced back to the state of Jalisco, where it was first created by ranchers as a hearty meal to fuel long days of work. Today though? Birria is a dish enjoyed throughout Mexico and beyond. I've even been able to find these tacos in London and as far as Manchester. It's absolutely not a good birria if you don't use dried Mexican chillies, which you can get online. If you're lucky enough to live near a Mexican market, they'll definitely have them. The chillies are what give this dish its vibrant colour and banging flayvas!

This is a dish that really feeds the soul. Now with these tacos, you dip the corn tortilla in the little bit of fat that forms from cooking the meat, fry lightly and stuff with cheese, that glorious meat, fresh onions and coriander. These tacos are sure to be a hit with even the pickiest eaters.

1 Remove the stems and seeds of the chillies and toast them in a dry pan over medium heat for a few minutes until fragrant. Remove and pop to the side.

2 In the same pan, heat 1 tablespoon of oil over medium heat and add the halved onion and the tomatoes. Brown them on all sides for about 5 minutes – this is where we actually work on developing flayva!

3 Then add the garlic cloves, oregano, thyme, cloves, peppercorns and carrot and cook for 2–4 minutes over low–medium heat to get all those ingredients acquainted. Remove from the heat.

4 Pat your short ribs and beef shank dry, season generously with the salt, cumin and black pepper on all sides.

5 In a large pot or Dutch oven, heat 2–3 tablespoons of oil over medium–high heat. Sear the meat on all sides (except the bottom of the ribs) – this should take about 2 minutes per side. This isn't a long sear, so the seasoning won't burn.

6 Transfer the meat, chillies and onion tomato mixture to a slow cooker or pressure cooker along with the beef stock. Pressure cook on high for 1 hour or slow cook on low for 6–8 hours. Alternatively, add the chillies, onion and tomato mixture and 800 ml (28 fl oz) beef stock to the pot with the meat and simmer, covered, over low heat for 2½–3 hours.

7   At this point the meat should fall/slide off the bone. If it's not, then allow it to cook a little more. Once your meat is tender and juicy, remove and shred with your hands or two forks. I know it's tempting but don't eat all the meat – I'm speaking from experience!

8   Skim any oil/fat from the surface of the cooking juices and save for later. Depending on the type of blender you have, you may not be able to blend hot liquids, so let the cooking juices cool and then blend everything with the apple cider vinegar and ginger.

9   Strain the mixture back into the pot and really push and squeeze out all that goodness. Discard the leftover bits as we've got every last drop of flayva out!

10 The consistency of your broth will vary as not everyone has the same power of heat source; if you used a slow cooker or pressure-cooked your meat, your cooking juices may be thin, which means you'll want to thicken them by bringing to the boil and reducing over medium heat. You want the consistency of a light soup or thin gravy. If it's too thick, add some water or beef stock to thin it out. Skim any remaining oil/fat from the surface and pop to the side with the rest from before.

11 At this point you can adjust the seasoning of your broth, if needed. Then coat your meat in a few spoonfuls – you want enough to keep it moist but the meat shouldn't be too sloppy and wet as it's going to fill your tacos.

12 Heat 1–2 teaspoons of the fat/oil in a pan over medium heat. Place a corn tortilla in the pan, cook for 30 seconds and flip. Then add a sprinkle of grated mozzarella on top, some shredded beef, 1 teaspoon of broth, a sprinkle of coriander and diced onion. If needed, drop the heat to low–medium as you don't want to burn your taco. Once assembled, fold your taco in half and cook until both sides are crispy and the cheese has melted. Repeat with all the tacos and filling. You can store the cooked tacos on a wire rack in an oven preheated to 90°C fan (225°F/Gas mark ¼) while making the rest.

13 Serve your tacos with a pot of broth, topped with onion, coriander and a squeeze of lime juice.

VEGAN BIRRIA TACOS

SERVES 2–4

vegetable oil, for frying
1.5 litres (52 fl oz) vegetable stock
2 onions: 1 halved, 1 finely diced
3 tomatoes
6 garlic cloves
2 tablespoons dried oregano,
  preferably Mexican
2 teaspoons fresh thyme leaves
3 cloves
1 teaspoon black peppercorns
1 carrot, peeled and halved
1 kg (2 lb 4 oz) king oyster
  mushrooms
2 x 400 g (14 oz) tins young jackfruit
1½ teaspoons salt
1 teaspoon mushroom salt
2 teaspoons ground cumin
2 teaspoons black pepper
2 tablespoons apple cider vinegar
½ teaspoon ground ginger
16–18 small corn tortillas
400 g (14 oz) vegan cheese, grated
  (I like smoked vegan Cheddar)
1 bunch of fresh coriander (cilantro),
  roughly chopped
3 limes, sliced into wedges

Chillies
2 guajillo
3 de arbol
2 ancho
1 chipotle
1 pasilla
1 mulato

When I created and developed my birria taco recipe (see pages 154–5), I just knew I had to veganise it. This recipe has fooled many, many people into thinking they were eating meat. So if you're looking to reduce your meat intake or just want to enjoy a meat-free version of birria tacos, look no further! Traditionally made with meat, in this recipe I've used mushrooms and jackfruit to get that perfect meat-like texture. I don't know how many times I've got to say this — if you're not using mushrooms as a meat substitute, what are you doing? Tell me! I would really like to know at this point. In this recipe we focus on king oyster mushrooms, not the clusters. King oyster mushrooms are great because they can easily be shredded using a fork, which creates a really meat-like texture. You can also use regular oyster mushrooms and shred them up too.

These tacos are perfect for any occasion, whether you're hosting a party or simply craving a delicious meal. They're easy to make and sure to impress any meat-lover with their flavour and texture. So, gather your ingredients and get ready to enjoy a vegan twist on this classic Mexican favourite!

1   Remove the stems and seeds of the chillies and toast them in a pan with 2 teaspoons of vegetable oil over medium heat for a few minutes until fragrant. Place into a pot over low heat with 750 ml (26 fl oz) of the vegetable stock. This will allow the chillies to infuse the stock while you prepare the remaining ingredients.

2   In the same pan you cooked the chillies, add the halved onion and tomatoes. Brown them on all sides for about 5 minutes – this is where we work on developing flayva!

3   Add the garlic cloves, oregano, thyme, cloves, peppercorns and carrot and cook over low–medium heat for 2–4 minutes to get all those ingredients acquainted. Then add to the pot with the chillies and another 750 ml (26 fl oz) vegetable stock. Simmer over low–medium heat for 1 hour.

4   While the broth is cooking away, shred the oyster mushrooms using a fork and place in a large bowl. Drain the jackfruit and use your hands to break it up into small chunks. Place in the bowl with the shredded mushrooms and season with the salt, mushroom salt (sub for regular salt if you don't have any), cumin and black pepper.

5   Using your hands, toss this mixture and then allow it to sit at room temperature for 30–35 minutes – this will draw out some of the moisture while also seasoning the mix. You will lose some mass from the mushrooms, but don't be alarmed. Using a muslin or clean cloth, squeeze the mushroom mixture. You don't want to squeeze until it's bone dry, just until the water is gone.

6   Depending on the type of blender you have, you may not be able to blend hot liquids, so let the cooking juices cool and then blend them with 2 teaspoons of oil, the apple cider vinegar and ginger. The reason we add oil is because traditionally this dish is made with meat that will release fat; however, the mushrooms and jackfruit won't do that.

7   Strain the mixture back into the pot and really push and squeeze out all of that goodness. Discard the leftover bits as we've got every last drop of flayva out!

8   The consistency of your broth will vary as not everyone has the same power of heat source. You want the consistency of a light soup or thin gravy. If it's too thin, allow it to simmer and reduce over medium heat. If it's too thick, add some water or vegetable stock to thin it out.

9   In a pan over medium–high heat, add 1 tablespoon of oil. Add the mushroom and jackfruit mixture to the pan – it should make that sizzle sound. After a few minutes, drop to medium heat and cook for 10 minutes, or until everything starts to crisp up and resemble shredded meat.

10 Add a few tablespoons of the broth to the mushroom and jackfruit mixture. We want it to be slightly moist, but not drowning in the sauce. Cook for another 2 minutes and pop to the side.

11 Heat 1–2 teaspoons of oil in a pan over medium heat. Quickly dip a corn tortilla into the broth and quickly place into the hot pan. Cook for 30 seconds and flip. Then add a sprinkle of grated vegan cheese on top, some shredded mushroom mix, 1 teaspoon of broth, a sprinkle of fresh coriander and diced onion. If needed, drop the heat to low–medium as you don't want to burn your taco. Once assembled, fold your taco in half and cook until both sides are crispy and the cheese has melted. Repeat with all the tacos and filling. You can store the cooked tacos on a wire rack in an oven preheated to 90°C fan (225°F/ Gas mark ¼) while making the rest.

12 Serve the tacos with a pot of broth, topped with onion, coriander and a squeeze of lime juice.

HOISIN MUSHROOM BARA TACOS

SERVES 4

Bara
250 g (9 oz) plain (all-purpose) flour
1 teaspoon salt
1 teaspoon instant yeast
½ teaspoon baking powder
¼ teaspoon ground turmeric
2¼ teaspoons dark soft brown sugar
200 ml (7 fl oz) warm water
oil

Mushroom filling
5 spring onions (scallions)
1 cucumber
1 kg (2 lb 4 oz) king oyster
   mushrooms or oyster mushrooms
2 tablespoons Chinese 5 spice
2 teaspoons white pepper
1–2 teaspoons salt
100 ml (3½ fl oz) vegetable oil
6 tablespoons cornflour (cornstarch)
6 tablespoons hoisin sauce, plus
   extra to serve
1 red chilli, sliced, to garnish

WHEN TRINI FLAYVAS MEET CHINESE FLAYVAS YOU GET A RECIPE LIKE THIS ONE. I think of these tacos as vegan duck pancakes but taken to the next level. I don't think you guys are really understanding the magic that I'm creating here...That's what this book is for though, to welcome you into my world of flayvas.

Baras are essentially a fried sort of flatbread; they're used for doubles (see page 135), which is a popular street food snack from Trinidad and Tobago. When I made this recipe, it was a happy accident. I had some bara left over along with a load of oyster mushrooms sitting in the refrigerator. If you don't know by now, mushrooms are the perfect meat substitute. The way you can manipulate them into tasting like anything is crazy. They soak up seasoning and sauces so well. They're not called king oyster mushrooms for no reason! I always say that I judge my vegan recipes the hardest, so trust me when I say this one is special.

1   For the bara (dough), combine all the dry ingredients in a bowl. Gradually add the warm water in four stages, kneading until combined. Your dough should still be sticky and soft – you don't want a tough dough.

2   Cover with 2 teaspoons of oil and allow to rest for 1 hour, or until doubled in size. Then split into 12 balls and allow to rest for another 30 minutes, or until doubled in size.

3   With lightly greased hands, spread the dough balls on a plate until they're nice and thin. In a heavy-bottomed pot, heat around 10–13 cm (4–5 inches) of oil to 175°C (345°F) and fry the bara for 10–15 seconds each side. They don't need long at all! Place into a container with a tea towel to catch the grease and keep them covered with a lid. The steam will help to keep the bara soft.

4   For the filling, julienne the spring onions, which means slice it thinly into strips. You want to slice your cucumber in half, remove the seeds and slice thinly, just like your spring onion, and pop to the side.

5   Use a fork to shred the king oyster mushrooms. If you're using just oyster mushrooms, you can use your hands to shred them into stringy pieces that resemble shredded chicken. Season with the 5 spice, white pepper and salt.

6   Heat the oil over medium heat; you want a good amount, so if your pan is quite large, add enough so you can shallow-fry. Working in batches, coat the mushrooms in the cornflour, then fry for 1–2 minutes, keeping them moving around and flipping if needed. Place the mushrooms on a tray lined with kitchen paper to catch any excess grease, then add the hoisin sauce and get that shredded mushroom coated in all of them flayvas!

7   Build the bara with some hoisin sauce, spring onion, cucumber, shredded mushroom and chilli slices to garnish. Bam.

JERK-SPICED CHICKEN QUESADILLAS

SERVES 4–6

600 g (1 lb 5 oz) boneless, skinless
  chicken thighs or 500 g (1 lb 2 oz)
  cooked chicken, chopped
2 teaspoons Dry Jerk Rub
  (page 208)
½ teaspoon salt
2–3 tablespoons vegetable oil
2 ripe plantains, peeled and cut into
  2 cm (¾ inch) cubes
4 large tortillas
200–250 g (7–9 oz) smoked
  Cheddar cheese, grated
sour cream, to serve (optional)
Mango Avocado Salad (page 112),
  to serve (optional)

Guacamole

1 small jalapeño chilli (charred,
  optional), diced
2 large avocados
¼ onion, diced
2 tablespoons chopped fresh
  coriander (cilantro)
1 tomato, deseeded and diced
2½ teaspoons fresh lime juice
½ teaspoon salt
¼ teaspoon ground cumin

Jerk sauce

1 tablespoon Wet Jerk Marinade
  (page 207)
225 g (8 oz) ketchup
150 g (5½ oz) honey
150 ml (5 fl oz) reduced-sodium
  chicken stock

Get ready to indulge in one of my first (at the time) viral and fusion recipes. When I started down the social media route, the aim was just to show people my cooking and creativity because at the time all I wanted was to bag a chef job and be taken seriously. This recipe is one of the dishes that changed the course of my journey. It's one of the easiest ultimate fusions of Jamaican and Mexican flavvas.

You can either use jerk chicken from a BBQ or whip up some jerk–spiced thighs — whatever you use will guarantee to hit differently! These quesadillas are packed with juicy, seasoned chicken and an addictive blend of spices. This twist on the classic dish is sure to become one of your new kitchen staples.

The bold and hearty jerk seasoning, traditionally used in Jamaican cuisine, pairs perfectly with the cheesy goodness of the quesadilla. And the best part? This recipe is easy to make, so you can enjoy restaurant–quality food in the comfort of your own home. You guys know I threw some plantain in this too. It's me after all! It's the perfect dish for any occasion, whether you're looking for a quick lunch or a satisfying dinner.

1   If you're using boneless chicken thighs, pat dry and season them with the dry jerk seasoning and salt. Allow to marinate while you make your guacamole and jerk sauce.

2   For the guacamole, add the jalapeño and avocados to a bowl and mash together. Mix in the remaining ingredients and keep refrigerated until ready to use.

3   To make the jerk sauce, combine all the ingredients in a small pot over medium heat. Bring to a simmer and cook for 5–7 minutes until slightly thickened. If it gets too thick, just add a little water to thin it out to your desired consistency.

4   For the plantain, heat the oil in a frying pan over medium heat. Once the oil is hot, add the plantains and fry for 3–5 minutes until golden brown, moving and turning regularly as they will cook quickly. Remove from the pan and set aside.

5   In the same pan, with the plantain-infused oil, sear the chicken thighs for 5–6 minutes per side or until they reach an internal temperature of 84°C (183°F). Allow to rest for 5 minutes before chopping up. Then coat in 150–200 ml (5–7 fl oz) of jerk sauce and set to the side. If you're using shredded cooked chicken, then toss the chicken in the pan over medium heat for a few minutes, then add the jerk sauce.

6   Lay out the tortillas on a clean work surface. Then, on one half, smear some guac, sprinkle with cheese, then with plantain and top evenly with cooked chicken. Add a small sprinkle of cheese on top of the chicken as this will act as a glue.

7   Fold the tortillas in half and press down gently, brush very lightly with oil. Heat a large frying pan or griddle pan over low–medium heat. Place the quesadillas in the pan and cook for 3–5 minutes on each side until the cheese is melted and the tortilla is crispy.

8   Serve the quesadillas with guacamole, sour cream, mango avocado salad or enjoy alone! Any remaining jerk sauce can be used as a dip or kept refrigerated for a week.

PHILLY 'JERK' STEAK

MAKES 4–6 CHEESESTEAKS

800 g (1 lb 12 oz) chuck or sirloin
   steak
2 onions
1 large green bell pepper (capsicum)
3–4 tablespoons vegetable oil
3 teaspoons Dry Jerk Rub
   (page 208)
8–12 slices of provolone or gouda
   cheese
4–6 white submarine rolls
butter, for spreading
salt
Scotch Bonnet Honey Sauce (page
   212) or mayo, to serve

Sweet jerk ketchup
200 g (7 oz) ketchup
200 ml (7 fl oz) chicken stock
   (reduced sodium) or water
100 ml (3½ fl oz) honey
1 tablespoon fresh lime juice
2 teaspoons Wet Jerk Marinade
   (page 207)

Now, if you're looking for a fusion recipe that's bursting with FLAYVAS, look no further. **This sandwich is a delicious combination of Caribbean and American flavours that will have your taste buds dancing.**

What makes this dish so rich in flavour is the combination of tender, juicy steak which has been seasoned with aromatic jerk seasoning, then topped with caramelised onions and peppers, melted cheese, and my signature Scotch bonnet honey sauce.

This is by no means an authentic Philly cheesesteak sandwich, but it's a beautiful Caribbean spin on one. This is perfect for those who are looking for a fakeaway option, as it can easily be made at home. It is a delicious, life-changing meal that brings together the best of both worlds. So, why not try it out and see for yourself?

We don't have Hoagie bread in the UK, so sub bread is your next best option here. If you can get your hands on some bread that isn't pre-sliced, that's great, as it's easier to make a little pocket for the meat.

1   Place the steak in the freezer for 20–25 minutes to enable the meat to firm up a little, which makes it easier to slice.

2   While your steak is in the freezer, now is a good time to make the sweet jerk ketchup. Trust me, it works. Bang all the sweet jerk ketchup ingredients in a pot. Stir until combined and bring to the boil, then simmer over medium heat for about 5 minutes until thickened. Pour the sauce into a bottle – it will keep in the refrigerator for 1–2 weeks.

3   Remove the steak from the freezer and cut into 5 mm (¼ inch) thick slices, against the grain. Start by identifying the direction of the grain. Look closely at the steak and you should be able to see the long, thin lines running through it. This is the grain. Once you've identified the grain, take a sharp knife and position it perpendicular to the direction of the grain. This means the blade should be running across the lines of the grain. Slice the onions and green pepper while you're there too.

4   Heat a large cast-iron or non-stick frying pan over medium heat and, once hot, add 2–3 tablespoons of oil, or enough to just cover the surface of your pan. Add the onions and green pepper to the pan, along with a sprinkle of salt. Cook for 2–3 minutes until the onions begin to soften and the pepper starts to brown on the edges. Remove from the pan.

5   The fun part! Make sure the pan is still nice and hot. If there's no
    oil left on the surface, add a likkle more. Sear the steak pieces over
    medium heat, you should hear a sizzle when it touches the pan.
    Don't overcrowd the pan, work in batches of two, if needed.
    If you overcrowd the pan, you'll just steam the steak. Season the
    steak with the dry jerk rub, a sprinkle of salt and press down so it
    gets into contact with the pan. Cook for 2–3 minutes, then flip and
    repeat the same process. Using a spatula or kitchen utensils, break
    the steak into smaller pieces, add the onions and pepper back into
    the mix and get them coated in the flavvas for a minute.

6   Split the steak mixture up so it's the same size as your bread
    rolls, then drizzle the sweet jerk ketchup over the steak; you only
    need 1–2 tablespoons as it shouldn't be crazy saucy. Add 2–3 slices
    of cheese per portion of steak and allow to melt by covering with
    a lid for a minute. Then remove from the heat and leave covered.

7   Toast the bread by opening it, spreading butter on the insides
    and toasting in a pan over medium heat until golden. Drizzle the
    insides with Scotch bonnet honey sauce, then using a large spatula,
    slot it under your meat and place it carefully into the bread rolls.
    Wrap in foil and slice down the middle to reveal that beautiful,
    cheesy goodness.

MONGOLIAN BEEF

SERVES 4—6

500 g (1 lb 2 oz) flank steak or
    bavette
80 ml (2½ fl oz) vegetable oil,
    plus 2 tablespoons
2 tablespoons light soy sauce
1½ tablespoons Shaoxing wine
½ teaspoon white pepper
¾ teaspoon bicarbonate of soda
    (baking soda)
30 g (1 oz) cornflour (cornstarch),
    plus 2 tablespoons
5 garlic cloves, minced
1 tablespoon minced fresh ginger
8 dried red Chinese chillies (optional)
4 spring onions (scallions), cut into
    2.5 cm (1 inch) pieces
toasted sesame seeds, to garnish
rice, to serve

Sauce
2 tablespoons soft dark or light
    brown sugar
1 teaspoon oyster sauce
180 ml (6 fl oz) reduced-sodium beef
    stock or water
3 tablespoons reduced-sodium light
    soy sauce
1 tablespoon cornflour (cornstarch)

THE DISH IS SO TENDER AND CRISPY I OFTEN HAVE TO STOP MYSELF FROM EATING THE BEEF BEFORE IT HITS THE SAUCE. **The sauce is what makes the dish so special, as it is rich with a perfect balance of flayva from the likes of soy sauce, oyster sauce and brown sugar. This recipe is ideal fakeaway inspiration for those who love Chinese takeout, as it is easy to make at home and can be customised to suit your taste preferences.**

I first tried this in America, it's not something I really see on menus in the UK, but we really are missing out because the ingredients are very easily sourced. Don't worry though, I'm here to come to the rescue and share these beautiful flayvas.

1. Alright, so the first thing you want to do is slice your steak against the grain. Start by identifying the direction of the grain. Look closely at the steak and you should be able to see the long, thin lines running through it. This is the grain. Once you've identified the grain, take a sharp knife and position it perpendicular to the direction of the grain. This means the blade should be running across the lines of the grain. Make a cut across the steak, slicing through it against the grain. Cut into 5 mm (¼ inch) thick slices and marinate with the 2 tablespoons of vegetable oil, the light soy sauce, Shaoxing wine, white pepper, bicarbonate of soda and the 2 tablespoons of cornflour for 15–20 minutes. **This is going to tenderise your meat!**

2. While you wait, combine the sugar, oyster sauce, beef stock, soy sauce and cornflour for the sauce in a bowl. Mix and pop to the side.

3. Now mix the beef; if you find it's a little dry, add 1 tablespoon of water to loosen it up. Then coat the beef in a bowl with the 30 g (1 oz) of cornflour, working in batches and ensuring you shake off any excess marinade.

4. Heat the 80 ml (2½ fl oz) vegetable oil in a wok and sear the beef for 1–2 minutes. Turn it over and let the other side sear for another 30 seconds–1 minute. Then remove from the heat and place on a tray lined with kitchen paper. At this point your beef should be golden, slightly brown and crispy.

5. Drain the oil, leaving 1–2 tablespoons in the wok. Over medium heat, fry the garlic and ginger for 15–30 seconds max, moving constantly so it doesn't burn. Then toss in the dried red chillies, if using. Stir-fry for another 30 seconds until the chillies are slightly toasted – they will also go from dark red to a more vibrant red.

6. Add the sauce, then give it a mix to ensure the cornflour hasn't settled. Stir to combine over medium heat, or until the sauce has thickened. **Bang in the beef and spring onions and get everything coated in them glorious flayvas!**

7. Serve immediately, garnished with the sesame seeds and enjoy with white rice.

HOT MUSHROOM FRIED SANDWICH

SERVES 4

4 clusters of oyster mushrooms,
  about 400–450 g (14 oz–1 lb),
  slightly smaller than your bun
vegetable oil, for frying
200 g (7 oz) Seasoned Flour
  (page 209)
4 vegan brioche buns
4 tablespoons vegan butter
large dill pickles, thickly sliced
  into rounds
shredded lettuce, to serve

Sauce
150 g (5½ oz) good-quality
  vegan mayonnaise
3 tablespoons ketchup
2 teaspoons American mustard
1 tablespoon vegan Worcestershire
  sauce
¾ teaspoon black pepper
pinch of salt

Vegan buttermilk
100 g (3½ oz) vegan Greek yogurt
130 ml (4 fl oz) almond milk
1 tablespoon fresh lemon juice

Maple hot sauce
60 ml (4 tablespoons) maple syrup
1 tablespoon cooking oil
2 teaspoons hot sauce
1 teaspoon dark soft brown sugar
1 teaspoon cayenne pepper

NOW, I KNOW YOU HAVEN'T TRIED A HOT MUSHROOM SANDWICH LIKE MINE. Over my career I've had a few recipes go viral and I've always felt the need to try and make those recipes veggie friendly. I develop dishes like these behind the scenes because they do take time and lots of it. I'm happy that I'm able to share this perfected version that's more inclusive for all.

To really get that convincing meat–like shape and texture, you want to use oyster mushroom clusters! The true flavvas are provided by that crispy, but perfectly seasoned coating. The spicy, spicy kick comes from the hot Nashville–style sauce that we brush over the mushrooms. The reason why I brush it over the mushrooms instead of dunking them in the sauce is so that they don't get all soggy and inedible.

Whether you're a vegan, vegetarian or simply looking to incorporate more veggies into your diet, this sandwich is sure to impress.

1   Okay, let's make the sauce for your sandwich. In a small bowl, mix together the vegan mayo, ketchup, American mustard, vegan Worcestershire sauce, pepper, and salt to taste. Keep refrigerated until ready to use.

2   To make the vegan buttermilk, mix the vegan Greek yogurt, almond milk and lemon juice together in a small bowl. Set aside for 10 minutes to thicken.

3   Brush off any debris from the mushrooms and make sure your clusters are just slightly smaller than your buns; they will gain some size from the coating.

4   In a large heavy-bottomed pot or Dutch oven, heat about 10 cm (4 inches) of oil to 175°C (345°F).

5   Place the seasoned flour in a bowl and coat the mushroom clusters in the flour one at a time. Then dip the mushrooms into the vegan buttermilk, shake off any excess and then coat them in the seasoned flour again. Carefully toss them side to side and ensure every nook and cranny is coated. Repeat with the remaining clusters and allow them to sit for 3 minutes before frying.

6   Fry the mushrooms for 3–4 minutes, turning halfway through, or until golden and crispy. Transfer to a kitchen paper-lined plate to drain any excess oil.

7   To make the maple hot sauce, combine all the ingredients in a small bowl and pop to the side.

8   Split the vegan brioche buns in half and spread each half with vegan butter. Toast the buns in a pan over medium–high heat until GOLDENNN.

9   To assemble the sandwiches, spread a generous amount of the mayo sauce on the bottom half of each bun. Then add pickles across the bottom, fried mushrooms, a drizzle of your maple hot sauce and top with shredded lettuce. Close with your top bun brushed with sauce. Serve immediately and thank me later.

SPECIAL FRIED RICE

SERVES 4

300 g (10½ oz) king prawns (jumbo shrimp), peeled and deveined
5 eggs
1 teaspoon white pepper
vegetable oil, for frying
2 ripe plantains (with a few spots of brown), diced into 1 cm (½ inch) cubes
4–6 spring onions (scallions), thinly sliced and whites and greens separated
5 garlic cloves, minced
1 teaspoon minced fresh ginger
750 g (1 lb 10 oz) cold cooked rice
2–3 tablespoons dark soy sauce
1 tablespoon ketchup
2 teaspoons oyster sauce
1 teaspoon chicken stock powder
1 teaspoon caster (superfine) sugar
1 teaspoon MSG (optional)
2 teaspoons toasted sesame oil
salt

NOW, THIS AIN'T YOUR EVERYDAY SPECIAL FRIED RICE. **It's special because it's a fusion dish... surprise, surprise! If you're looking for a unique twist on a traditional rice dish, then this is the one for you. While it may not be the most authentic Jamaican or Chinese dish out there, it combines the best of both worlds with fusion flavvas that will tantalise your taste buds.**

The star of the show is the plantain, a staple ingredient in Jamaican cuisine. **By adding it to the mix, we've elevated the dish to a whole new level of yum. This special fried plantain rice is inspired by fakeaway culture, where you can indulge in your favourite takeout choices without having to leave your house. So get ready to savour the unique blend of Jamaican and Chinese influences in every bite.**

1   First, rinse the prawns under cold water, pat dry and season with a lil salt.

2   Whisk the eggs, half the white pepper and a little salt. I don't usually recommend salting eggs for scrambled eggs, but these ones are very different to breakfast eggs. Pop to the side.

3   Heat 4–5 tablespoons of oil in a wok over medium heat and fry the plantain cubes for about 3 minutes, moving and turning regularly until golden brown. Reduce the heat if needed, as woks heat up extremely quickly. Once cooked, remove to a bowl and pop to the side.

4   Leave 2–3 tablespoons of oil in your wok, or add more oil so you have this amount, and fry the prawns over medium heat for 1–2 minutes. You don't need to cook these completely as the prawns will continue to cook when we add them back in later on. Remove from the pan and place to the side.

5   Turn up the heat to medium–high. Add the eggs, stir and let the mixture sit for 15–30 seconds, then break up and cook until golden and separated. Drop the heat to medium, push the eggs to the side and add the spring onion whites, garlic and ginger. Cook for 1–2 minutes, moving around in the oil.

6   Now add the rice into the wok, season with the soy sauce, ketchup, oyster sauce, chicken stock powder, sugar, the remaining white pepper and MSG (if using). Mix all your ingredients together. Increase the heat to high, toss and get your rice nice and hot.

7   Cook for 2 minutes, then add the plantain and prawns, spring onion greens and sesame oil and sauté for another 1–2 minutes.

8   Serve and enjoy these fusion flavvas!

SWE
TING

I'm one of those people that ALWAYS has room for dessert. We all know that your dessert belly is separate from your main belly. Saying that, I feel like I've grown out of my sweet tooth because I used to have sweets every day, but now for me to have something sweet, it needs to be worth it. Is this chapter worth it? ABSOLUTELY. I'm also the type of person that HAS to have something sweet after Sunday dinner, because would it really be Sunday dinner if you didn't have dessert? No it wouldn't!

Now, it's taken a lot for me to share these recipes – I really don't mind sharing my savoury recipes but because baking isn't my speciality, so much testing goes into getting the sweet tings right! I truly believe there is something for everyone in this section – even the 'hardest' recipes are still pretty easy. I even decided to include a few drinks recipes because sometimes you don't actually want a dessert that you have to eat, sometimes that craving is satisfied by a sweet drink.

GINGER TOFFEE SPICED PUDDING

SERVES 6

95 g (3¼ oz) butter, softened, plus
    extra for greasing
150 g (5½ oz) dark soft brown sugar
2 eggs, at room temperature
2 tablespoons black treacle
1 teaspoon vanilla bean paste
    or extract
60 g (2¼ oz) minced stem ginger
    in syrup
1 tablespoon stem ginger syrup
1 teaspoon ground ginger
¾ teaspoon bicarbonate of soda
    (baking soda)
pinch of salt
180 g (6 oz) self-raising flour
100 ml (3½ fl oz) cold black tea
Nutmeg Ice Cream (page 190)
    or custard, to serve

Toffee sauce
150 g (5½ oz) dark soft brown sugar
60 g (2¼ oz) butter
2 teaspoons black treacle
200 ml (7 fl oz) double
    (heavy) cream
pinch of salt

THINK OF THIS ONE AS A STICKY TOFFEE PUDDING SORT OF SITUATION BUT TAKEN TO THE NEXT LEVEL. **Just as easy to make but the addition of sweet sticky stem ginger has this dessert hitting differently. When it comes to desserts, this is my favourite one of all time. I'm a proper pudding person. It's been ingrained in me from a young age and if I ever see sticky toffee pudding on a menu, you best believe I'm getting that!**

Now, just because it's easy to make, it doesn't mean everyone gets it right. The one thing I despise about traditional sticky toffee pudding is the dates — I can't stand them unless they're blended up. So when I created this recipe, I thought about the things I love and flavvas I love, that would work together to add my own spin on a classic. I can't lie, it took me a while to get the sponge right, because it has to have that spring to it while not being dry. I got there in the end after a few ear tantrums and a belly full of sticky ginger pudding.

I like to make this recipe in small individual pudding pots — it's easier, it's quicker and requires less time in the oven — but you can bang this in a small tin too.

1   Preheat the oven to 180°C fan (400°F/Gas mark 6).

2   In a stand mixer or bowl, beat together the butter and sugar on medium speed, ensuring you scrape down the sides. You want to do this until it's a shade lighter than when first combined together. This will take about 4 minutes by hand and 2 minutes in a mixer. Don't be that person and skip this step because it's what helps to make the sponge light and fluffy!

3   Add the eggs, one at a time, and continue to mix until just combined – this only takes a minute. Add the black treacle, vanilla, stem ginger, ginger syrup, ground ginger, bicarbonate of soda and salt. Give it a good mix for 1 minute. Now fold in the flour. Once combined and no streaks remain, mix in the cold black tea.

4   Use your fingers to grease 6 pudding moulds with a little butter and add the mixture to the moulds. Leave 1 cm (½ inch) from the rim to allow the pudding to rise. Then place on a baking tray and bake for 20–22 minutes.

5   While the puddings bake, grab a pan and melt the sugar, butter and treacle over medium heat. Once it's melted and resembles the consistency of syrup, add the cream and mix. After 1–2 minutes the sauce will have thickened. Finish with the salt.

6   You'll know the sponge is done when you can slide a butter knife in and no streaks or cake batter stick to it.

7   I personally like to serve these puddings with a scoop of nutmeg ice cream and drizzle the toffee sauce on top, but you can also have them with custard.

VEGAN CINNAMON ROLLS

MAKES 12–15

Dough
45 g (1½ oz) vegan butter, plus
   extra for greasing
250 ml (9 fl oz) almond milk
1 tablespoon dark soft brown sugar
1 teaspoon vanilla bean paste
   or extract
pinch of salt
1 packet of instant yeast
   (2½ teaspoons)
400 g (14 oz) plain (all-purpose)
   flour, plus extra for dusting
1 teaspoon vegetable oil

Filling
130 g (4½ oz) salted vegan butter,
   softened (unsalted will still be fine)
250 g (9 oz) dark soft brown sugar
2 tablespoons ground cinnamon

Frosting
75 g (2½ oz) salted vegan butter,
   softened
170 g (6 oz) vegan cream cheese
250 g (9 oz) icing (confectioners')
   sugar, sifted
1 teaspoon maple syrup
¼ teaspoon ground cinnamon
1 teaspoon vanilla bean paste
   or extract

NOW THIS RECIPE IS MY BABY, I thought long and hard about sharing this one. Then I realised that these cinnamon rolls are simply too good not to share. They are gooey, moist, sweet in all the right places and completely VEGAN.

When I made this recipe, I didn't think it was possible to fall in love with a cinnamon roll. I know people find baking daunting, but I'm telling you it's really simple. It may take a few hours, but it's totally worth it! The dough is very simple to make, the important part is understanding the yeast you're using and when to add it. Always double check this before going ahead with the recipe steps. Secondly, the dough needs to rise. If your kitchen isn't warm, then simply turn your oven on full blast for 2 minutes, then turn it off and place your dough in the oven to rise (after 10 minutes). This creates the perfect warm temperature for your dough to rise.

Vegan baking was pretty hard to do up until recently. You can now get vegan butter and I absolutely swear by it. You can get butter blocks that come in salted and unsalted variations. Now, these cinnamon rolls are amazing without the frosting, but they absolutely blow your mind when it's added. **You can also use a simple frosting too.**

1   For the dough, heat the vegan butter and almond milk together in a heatproof bowl in the microwave in short bursts of 15–30 seconds until warm (35–40°C/95–105°F).

2   Add the sugar, vanilla, salt and yeast. Depending on the type of yeast you're using, you may need to prove it. Now you want to give it all a mix and gradually add the flour using a wooden spoon. Only do this until the dough has just combined. Then knead the dough for 5 minutes, or until smooth, by hand.

3   Once smooth, add the dough to a lightly oiled bowl, and lightly oil the dough too. Cover with cling film (plastic wrap) and allow to rise somewhere warm for 45 minutes–1 hour, or until doubled in size. If you're making these on a warm day, the countertop will do.

4   While the dough is rising, combine the vegan butter, sugar and cinnamon for the filling. Mix until smooth. Before rolling out the dough, lightly flour the work surface to ensure the dough doesn't stick when rolling it out.

continued overleaf

5   Roll out the dough into a thin rectangle about 5 mm (¼ inch) thick. **Evenly spread the filling across the surface – don't be shy!** Make sure you get the edges too. Starting at the longest end of the dough, tightly roll up the dough. It's absolutely crucial that you roll tightly. Then, with a serrated knife or a string of floss, cut the dough into 4–5 cm (1½–2 inch) sections. Transfer to a lightly buttered tin, cover and leave to rise for 40 minutes in a warm spot.

6   Preheat the oven to 170°C fan (375°F/Gas mark 5).

7   Bake the rolls in the centre of the oven for 25–30 minutes. If you notice at the 15-minute mark that the rolls are getting too brown, cover them with foil. This should be the only time you open the oven to check them!

8   To make the frosting, combine the vegan butter and vegan cream cheese. Then gradually add the icing sugar. Once combined, mix in the maple syrup, cinnamon and vanilla.

9   Remove the cinnamon rolls from the oven. The key to gooey cinnamon rolls is to add half the frosting while warm and the other half once they've cooled down.

HARDO BREAD FRENCH TOAST

SERVES 2–4

2 eggs
150 ml (5 fl oz) full-fat cow's milk
  or plant-based milk
50 ml (3½ tablespoons) double
  (heavy) cream or plant-based
  cream
2 teaspoons vanilla bean paste
  or extract
1½ teaspoons caster (superfine)
  sugar
1 teaspoon ground cinnamon
½ teaspoon freshly grated nutmeg
vegetable oil or butter, for frying
8 x 2 cm (¾ inch) thick slices of
  hardo/sweet Jamaican bread

To serve
butter (optional)
maple syrup or honey
raspberries and blueberries
icing (confectioners') sugar

Introducing the perfect but simple sweet fusion of Jamaican and American flayvas — hardo bread French toast! This easy recipe will get you hooked. Most people have French toast for breakfast, but I am not most people, okay? I love this recipe because hardo bread is a little dense, yet its sweet and soft texture makes it perfect for French toast. Similar to traditional French toast, this dish is made by soaking thick slices of hardo bread in a custard–like mixture of eggs, milk and spices before cooking to golden perfection.

The result is a deliciously sweet and fluffy dessert (or breakfast) treat that will leave you craving more and more and more. I really enjoy this recipe with my nutmeg ice cream (page 190); it's the perfect combo that will never EVER let you down. Whether you're looking to switch up your breakfast routine or want to impress your guests with a unique twist on a classic dish, this French toast is sure to be a crowd–pleaser. So whip up a batch and enjoy.

1   To make the custard, whisk together the eggs, milk, cream, vanilla, sugar, cinnamon and nutmeg until well combined.

2   Heat about 1 tablespoon of oil or butter in a large frying pan over low–medium heat.

3   Dip each slice of hardo bread into the egg mixture, making sure to coat both sides evenly, you want to let it sit in the mixture for 10–15 seconds or just until the bread starts to feel squidgy on the outside but still a little firm. Hardo bread is dense, so you want to make sure it soaks up some of that mixture.

4   Place the coated bread slices into the frying pan and cook for 2–3 minutes on each side, or until golden brown and crispy. You should be able to fit two pieces in your pan. If using butter, you want to wipe the pan after each use because it will eventually start to burn and get smoky.

5   To work in batches, preheat the oven to 90°C fan (225°F/Gas mark ¼) and use it to keep your French toast warm while you prepare the rest.

6   Once all the bread slices are cooked, serve immediately with some butter, maple syrup, berries and a dusting of icing sugar so you can feel fancy!

BOOZY BANANA BREAD

SERVES 8

2–3 ripe bananas (about 230 g/
  8½ oz)
55 g (2 oz) buttermilk or sour cream
2 large eggs, at room temperature
1 teaspoon vanilla bean paste
115 ml (3¾ fl oz) vegetable oil
150 g (5½ oz) caster (superfine)
  sugar
100 g (3½ oz) dark soft brown sugar
250 g (9 oz) plain (all-purpose) flour
1 teaspoon baking powder
½ teaspoon bicarbonate of soda
  (baking soda)
½ teaspoon freshly grated nutmeg
1 teaspoon ground cinnamon
¼ teaspoon ground allspice

Frosting
200 g (7 oz) cream cheese
3 tablespoons salted butter, softened
350 g (12 oz) icing (confectioners')
  sugar
2½ tablespoons Disaronno
zest of 1 lime

Have you ever made something so good you didn't want to share it? Well, for me, this is one of those recipes. Don't get me wrong, all my recipes are top notch, but this one? It never fails me and it's pretty foolproof. I think baking can be a little daunting, but this recipe isn't. The flayvas taste complex, but I purposely made this recipe as easy to follow as possible. Yeah, it's a banana bread, but this one's simple. I think the icing is a great touch but if you don't have much of a sweet tooth and want to keep it plain, then you can't beat a slice of banana bread toasted in a pan with a little butter, then topped with ice cream. It's a great way to use leftovers (if you have any!).

The key to moist banana cake is yogurt. You also want to make sure you're using ripe bananas, and for me that's never hard because I always have a few bananas that are just way too ripe to consume as a snack. With this banana cake you'll really taste the Caribbean flavours. We season everything and it's no different with cake. Nutmeg, cinnamon, allspice and vanilla are what takes your banana bread to the next level, just trust me.

Now, I'm using a 23 x 13 cm (9 x 5 inch) loaf tin, your tin doesn't have to be the exact same size but please remember if you use a smaller tin, it will take longer to cook and if you use a larger tin, it will take less time. If your tin isn't non-stick, then ensure that you lightly grease the loaf tin and/or line it with non-stick baking parchment.

1 Preheat the oven to 170°C fan (375°F/Gas mark 5) and line or grease a 23 x 13 cm (9 x 5 inch) loaf tin if it isn't non-stick.

2 In a bowl, beat and mash together the bananas. Then add the buttermilk, eggs, vanilla, oil and both sugars. Whisk until combined.

3 Add the remaining dry ingredients to the bowl and mix until just combined. Once the streaks are gone, stop mixing. The whole mixing process should take no longer than 1–2 minutes.

4 Carefully pour the mixture into the prepared loaf tin, making sure it's level to ensure even baking. Place onto the centre shelf of the oven and bake for 1 hour–1 hour 10 minutes, or until golden and you can poke a butter knife or toothpick into the middle and it comes out with a few crumbs. Allow your banana bread to cool in the tin for 15 minutes before transferring to a wire rack.

5 To make the frosting, beat the cream cheese and butter until combined, then add the icing sugar, Disaronno and lime zest and mix until nicely incorporated. Keep refrigerated until you're ready to use.

6 Once the banana bread has cooled, you can either spread the frosting over with a spatula or pipe it on if you're feeling fancy!

CHEWY CHOCOLATE CHIP TOFFEE COOKIES

MAKES 20—24

375 g (13 oz) plain (all-purpose) flour
1 teaspoon bicarbonate of soda (baking soda)
½ teaspoon salt
225 g (8 oz) butter, at room temperature
250 g (9 oz) light soft brown sugar
150 g (5½ oz) granulated sugar
2 large eggs, at room temperature
1 teaspoon vanilla extract
150 g (5½ oz) milk chocolate chips
150 g (5½ oz) 60% cocoa chocolate, cut into chunks
20–24 soft toffee sweets
flaky salt, for sprinkling

Now, I'm not really a huge chocolate fan, but there's one thing that involves chocolate that does drive me crazy and that's fresh, warm, gooey chocolate chip cookies! I'm not even being dramatic when I say I'm literally drooling at the thought of a warm chocolate chip cookie with some vanilla milk...

The purpose of this recipe is that it's easy. There's recipes out there that require you to brown butter and chill the dough for extended periods, and that's great but sometimes I crave cookies on a random Saturday and want to be able to have them in an hour. Some recipes call for an extra egg yolk or two and I used to do this, but then I was left with egg whites that I didn't really want, so I tested and tested and got this creation. Oh, and the wonderful thing about this recipe is that you can make the cookies and freeze the dough, so I usually make these cookies, freeze a few balls in a Ziplock bag and just pull a ball or two out when I need to satisfy that cookie craving. The dough lasts for 3 months; it'll probably keep for longer but I wouldn't be able to tell you as it never lasts that long in my house.

I can't stress this enough: use room temperature ingredients and measure them carefully. You can't blame me if your recipe fails because you thought eyeballing it would get you somewhere! Let's work smart now people! The reason for ensuring you use room temperature ingredients is because we all know butter is rock hard straight out the refrigerator and we beat the butter in this recipe — you can try beating rock hard butter but you won't get far. Beating the butter in this recipe creates air, which contributes to a more even cookie. The same goes for the eggs — room temperature eggs contribute towards fluffier cookies. Everything in this recipe has been measured to a T to create that chewy cookie which everybody loves.

1   In a medium bowl, whisk together the flour, bicarbonate of soda and salt. Pop to the side.

2   Add the butter and both sugars to a stand mixer. Beat on medium speed for 3 minutes until light and fluffy. I use a stand mixer because I have one, but if you don't, you're gonna need to put in some work and beat the hell out of the butter for at least 5 minutes. I'm not judging you if you need to take breaks, don't worry. Be sure to scrape down the sides of your bowl every now and then. If it's not pale in colour and light in texture, you need to go a little longer.

3   Next, add the eggs and vanilla and beat until just combined. This won't take long, but be sure to scrape down the sides again as you don't want to miss any mixture. Remember your flour from earlier? Add this into the bowl and mix on low speed until combined; there should be no streaks or dry spots of flour. Don't overmix the dough – we're making cookies, not bread. Overmixing will develop the gluten in the flour too much.

4   Bang in the chocolate chips and chopped chocolate and fold them in. The mix for me is perfect because a good-quality chopped chocolate creates little pools of melted chocolate in the cookies.

5   Preheat the oven to 170°C fan (375°F/Gas mark 5).

6   While the oven heats up, place the cookie dough in the refrigerator for 20–25 minutes.

7   Now grab a golf-ball-sized amount of dough and flatten with your hand. Add a toffee sweet to the middle and seal the edges, shaping the dough into a ball. Place onto a lined baking sheet. Repeat the process with the rest of your dough and ensure there's at least 7.5 cm (3 inches) between each cookie, as they will spread during baking.

8   Bake for 10–12 minutes, the edges should be nice and golden. Check at the 10-minute mark. The cookies will continue to cook once they leave the oven, so don't worry if the centre is a little light in colour or soft-looking.

9   Tip tap your tray on the work surface once to deflate your cookies, as they will look kinda puffy at this point. Then allow them to cool on the tray for at least 10 minutes. As they cool, they'll change in appearance, cracks will appear on the surface and the edges will start to harden. Trust the process.

10 Transfer the cookies to a wire rack, sprinkle with some flaky salt and enjoy warm.

SUPER MOIST DOUGHNUTS

MAKES 12

425 g (15 oz) bread flour
55 g (2 oz) caster (superfine) sugar,
  plus extra for dusting
8 g (¼ oz) active dried yeast
¾ teaspoon salt
½ teaspoon freshly grated nutmeg
  (optional)
180 ml (6 fl oz) warm milk
  (34–38°C/93–100°F)
1 teaspoon vanilla bean paste
1 large egg
1 egg yolk
65 g (2¼ oz) butter, at room
  temperature
vegetable oil, for frying

Filling
500 ml (17 fl oz) Coconut Custard
  (page 193)
200 ml (7 fl oz) double (heavy)
  cream
2 tablespoons caster (superfine)
  sugar
good-quality raspberry jam

LOOKING FOR A PERFECT AND SUPER MOIST DOUGHNUT RECIPE?
You know I've got you. These doughnuts are the ultimate treat with their soft and tender texture and sweet addictive taste. When I created this recipe, I thought I'd cracked the code. Then I wasn't sure if I should even share this recipe because I didn't want a certain doughnut chain to come for me!

These doughnuts will have you reaching for seconds (and maybe even thirds). I can't lie, I don't know if you'll make it to the filling part without demolishing a few. The secret to these doughnuts is treating them like bread. For me, a good doughnut needs yeast because it creates that perfect bite. I'm a simple man when it comes to doughnuts but I pushed the boat out with this one and wasn't disappointed, let me tell ya!

Serve them up with a hot cup of coffee or tea and enjoy the perfect balance. Get started on making these tasty doughnuts today and indulge — because I know I did.

1   Okay, so in a stand mixer bowl, add the flour, sugar, yeast, salt and nutmeg (if using). Mix so the ingredients are evenly dispersed. Then combine the warm milk with the vanilla, egg and egg yolk. You really need to ensure the milk is warm to the touch and not hot. Yeast thrives in warm temperatures, so if the milk is too hot, you'll kill your yeast and scramble your eggs.

2   Combine the milk mixture with the dry ingredients and mix for 5 minutes on medium speed. While your dough is mixing, cut your butter into cubes.

3   Add the cubes of butter into the dough gradually and mix for another 8–10 minutes. The dough should be smooth and slightly sticky. Just trust the process, it will look very sticky at the beginning.

4   Place the dough in a clean bowl and cover with cling film (plastic wrap) and/or a clean damp tea towel. Leave to prove for 1–2 hours, or until your dough has doubled in size. If your kitchen is cold, a great tip that will help is turning your oven on full blast for a minute, then turning it off. Let your dough prove in the oven as it creates the perfect warm environment. Or you can just leave your oven light on, that works too!

5   While the dough is proving, cut twelve 10–13 cm (4–5 inch) squares of baking parchment.

6   Once the dough doubles in size, punch it down, then split into 12 pieces. For precision, you can weigh the dough and split it into equal pieces.

continued overleaf

7   Now flatten a piece of dough and tuck the edges into the centre, flip the dough over so the seam touches the surface, then make a claw-like shape over your dough so you're cupping the dough. Roll the dough around so you shape it into a perfect circle, then place on a square of baking parchment. Repeat with the remaining pieces of dough. Leave to prove in a warm spot for 40–50 minutes, or until doubled in size again.

8   Heat a heavy-bottomed pot or Dutch oven with plenty of vegetable oil, roughly halfway up the sides of your pot. Once the oil reaches 170°C (340°F), carefully place the doughnuts into the oil, baking parchment side first. Use tongs to remove the baking parchment and fry for 1–2 minutes per side. Use a slotted spoon to remove them from the oil and place on a kitchen paper-lined tray to catch any excess grease.

9   Repeat until all doughnuts are done. Remember, don't overcrowd the pot.

10 While your doughnuts are cooling, place your coconut custard in a bowl. In a separate bowl, whip your double cream and caster sugar together until thick. Fold your double cream into your custard.

11 Once the doughnuts have cooled a lil (enough for you to handle), place them in a bowl with some caster sugar and coat 1–2 at a time. Then insert a chopstick or butter knife into the centre and wiggle side to side, this will be your pocket for the fillings.

12 Place your custard filling into a piping bag and the raspberry jam into a separate piping bag. Now you can fill your doughnuts with raspberry jam or the coconut custard. I like to mix it up. To pipe your fillings inside, place the nozzle in and gently squeeze until your doughnut starts to fill and some of the jam or custard can be seen at the entrance.

SWEET FRITTERS

SERVES 4

3 overripe bananas or 2 very
  ripe plantains
150 ml (5 fl oz) coconut milk
100 ml (3½ fl oz) oat milk
1 egg
7 tablespoons light soft brown sugar
1 tablespoon vanilla bean paste
  or extract
300 g (10½ oz) plain (all-purpose)
  flour
1 tablespoon baking powder
2 teaspoons ground cinnamon
1 teaspoon freshly grated nutmeg
½ teaspoon salt
vegetable oil, for frying

Ginger-infused rum honey
150 g (5½ oz) good-quality honey
2½ teaspoons grated fresh ginger
½ teaspoon ground ginger
1 tablespoon white rum

To serve
nutmeg or vanilla ice cream
  (see page 190 for homemade)
crumbled ginger biscuits

These banana fritters are the perfect solution for using up old overripe bananas, while also satisfying your sweet tooth. This easy and creamy recipe is influenced by my Jamaican roots and when I was little, I would save my bananas from packed lunches and let them get ripe so I could have these! Sorry, Mum.

For me, these fritters really capture the true essence of Jamaican cuisine, which is no-waste cooking with maximum flavvas! **Imagine a stack of pancake-like fritters with crispy edges and a soft, warm centre that will melt in your mouth with each bite. To take these fritters to the next level, drizzle with a ginger-infused rum honey, which adds a sweet and spicy taste that will have you absolutely hooked. I also like to add a scoop of my good old nutmeg ice cream (page 190). This recipe is a must-try for anyone looking to indulge in a tasty, unique and easy treat.**

1   For the honey, combine the honey and both gingers. Simmer over low heat for 5–10 minutes – you don't want to boil this at all. The aroma of ginger should be present. Remove from the heat, add the rum and stir. Allow to cool while you make your fritter batter.

2   For the fritters, peel and mash the overripe bananas in a mixing bowl. Add the coconut milk, oat milk, egg, sugar and vanilla. Stir the mixture until it is well combined.

3   In a separate mixing bowl, whisk together the flour, baking powder, cinnamon, nutmeg and salt. Add the dry ingredients to the banana mixture and stir until combined. Be careful not to overmix, but there should be no streaks of flour. Allow the ingredients to soak up the flour for 20 minutes.

4   Heat 1 tablespoon of oil in a large frying pan over low–medium heat – you basically need just enough to cover the base of the pan with a thin layer.

5   Pour the batter into the hot oil – around 4 tablespoons should do. I like to make circles, but you can keep it rustic. Fry the fritters for 2–3 minutes on each side, or until they are golden brown; you'll know it's time to flip them when you see some bubbles on the surface of the fritter. You should be able to cook 2–3 fritters at a time.

6   Use a slotted spoon to remove the fritters from the pan and place them on a kitchen paper-lined plate to drain any excess oil. Then continue to fry your fritters, adding a little oil for each batch if needed. If your pan is dry, your fritters won't get that crispy, almost caramelised crust that everybody knows and loves! If you find that after flipping your fritters, the edges are dry, add a few drops of oil and that will get them crispy, too.

7   Serve the fritters warm with the ginger-infused rum honey drizzled on top and nutmeg or vanilla ice cream. I also like to add some crumbled ginger biscuits because I'm a textures man!

CARAMEL APPLE CRUMBLE CAKE

SERVES 8–10

300 g (10½ oz) plain (all-purpose)
  flour
1 teaspoon bicarbonate of soda
  (baking soda)
½ teaspoon baking powder
pinch of salt
225 g (8 oz) granulated sugar
165 g (5¾ oz) butter, softened,
  plus extra for greasing
3 eggs, at room temperature
200 g (7 oz) sour cream, at room
  temperature
1 tablespoon vanilla bean paste or
  vanilla extract
Salted Caramel (page 189),
  for drizzling
icing (confectioners') sugar,
  for dusting

Crumble topping
300 g (10½ oz) plain (all-purpose)
  flour
300 g (10½ oz) granulated sugar
100 g (3½ oz) dark soft brown sugar
2½ teaspoons ground cinnamon
1 teaspoon freshly grated nutmeg
pinch of salt
225 g (8 oz) butter, melted

Brown butter apple topping
3 tablespoons butter
3 tablespoons light soft brown sugar
½ teaspoon ground cinnamon
pinch of freshly grated nutmeg
pinch of salt
2 large Granny Smith apples, cut into
  1 cm (½ inch) chunks or sliced

CARAMEL, APPLE, CRUMBLE AND CAKE. **A combo that makes a lot of sense. I absolutely love apple crumble, it's one of my favourite desserts, and I really appreciate a nice sponge cake, so when I combined these two, I knew it would be a hit. It doesn't require crazy skills or the fanciest of equipment and it's not about showing off. This is the type of dessert you can enjoy with a good old cup of tea (preferably Yorkshire).**

1   Alright, so you want to make the crumble topping by mixing the flour, both sugars, the cinnamon, nutmeg and salt together in a large bowl. Then stir in the melted, but slightly cooled, butter. Use a fork to mix and you'll see it start to resemble crumbs. Use your hands to clump a few pieces together to form crumbs too. Pop to the side.

2   Preheat the oven to 175°C fan (385°F/Gas mark 5½). Grease a 23 x 33 cm (9 x 13 inch) baking tin or line with baking parchment to be safe.

3   For the apple topping, add the butter to a medium pot over medium heat. Cook for 2–3 minutes, or until the butter starts to brown and little specks of brown are present. Then drop the heat to low and add the sugar, cinnamon, nutmeg and salt. Once combined, toss in the apples and coat. We aren't aiming to cook the apples at this point. Allow to cool while you prepare the cake.

4   In a medium bowl, combine the flour, bicarbonate of soda, baking powder and salt. Whisk and pop to the side.

5   Now, I use a stand mixer but you can use a hand-held mixer or your arm strength, but that will take a little longer! Using a stand mixer fitted with the paddle attachment, beat the sugar and butter for 2–4 minutes until light and pale in colour. Be sure to scrape down the sides of the bowl after every step, getting the bottom of the bowl too.

6   Add the eggs, one at a time, on medium speed, scrape down the sides, then add the sour cream and vanilla and beat on medium speed until combined. At this point it will look like you've messed up, as it just looks like a curdled accident, but don't worry, you haven't!

7   On low speed, add the dry ingredients and mix until no more flour streaks are present, but don't overmix!

8   Pour the batter into your prepared tin, then evenly coat with the brown butter apples, then the crumble topping. Lightly press down so the crumble sticks. Bake for 45 minutes–1 hour. Baking times do vary, so keep an eye on it. A toothpick inserted into the centre should have a small number of moist crumbs, not wet batter. You don't want your toothpick coming out dry, especially since there's apples that should be moist in there. If you find it's getting dark at the 30-minute mark, cover it loosely with foil.

9   Allow to cool in the tin for 45 minutes–1 hour, then drizzle with salted caramel and dust with icing sugar to serve.

GINGER GUAVA CHEESECAKE

SERVES 10

Base
400 g (14 oz) ginger biscuits
½ teaspoon ground cardamom
1 teaspoon ground ginger
pinch of salt
100 g (3½ oz) plus
    1 tablespoon butter, melted,
    plus extra for greasing

Cheesecake filling
700 g (1 lb 9 oz) cream cheese,
    softened at room temperature
260 g (9¼ oz) caster (superfine)
    sugar
4 eggs
170 g (6 oz) double (heavy) cream
2 teaspoons vanilla bean paste
    or extract
½ teaspoon orange flavouring
½ teaspoon ground ginger

Glaze
300 g (10½ oz) guava jam
1 teaspoon apple juice
1 teaspoon fresh lime juice

ALL MY DESSERTS ARE CLOSE TO MY HEART, BUT THIS ONE IS EXTRA SPECIAL because it took me so long to perfect my cheesecake filling to a standard that could be replicated. I love a no-bake cheesecake, but the flayvas and texture of a baked cheesecake just can't be compared. With a ginger biscuit crust and a unique Caribbean flair, this dessert is a true flayva experience. The delicate balance of spicy ginger and sweet guava creates a taste sensation that will leave you speechless.

I'm a little fussy when it comes to food and I've finally accepted that... begrudgingly. I really like to bring the crusts of the cheesecake up because then every single bite has the banging ginger crust and then some. And let's not forget about the guava, it really takes this cheesecake from good to amazing. This fruit has been enjoyed in the Caribbean for centuries, and it's known for its sweet and tangy flavour. Paired with the slight spicy kick of ginger? Yeah, I need a prize for this or something. You can order guava jam online, but most supermarkets will have it in their selection of Afro-Caribbean products and you'll definitely find it in any Caribbean market you go to. This dessert is truly a unique and unforgettable experience that will transport you straight to the islands, for a considerably smaller fee than flying.

1   Preheat the oven to 140°C fan (325°F/Gas mark 3). Grease the sides of a 23 cm (9 inch) springform tin with some butter or oil and line the bottom with baking parchment.

2   In a food processor, crush the ginger biscuits into fine crumbs or place your biscuits in a Ziplock bag and use a rolling pin to bash them. Then pour into a bowl and mix in the cardamom, ginger, salt and melted butter. Mix until combined – the biscuit crumbs should be able to clump together if you squeeze them, but still easily break apart if you smush them.

3   Pour the biscuit mixture into the prepared tin and use a flat-bottomed glass to press the mixture firmly into the base. Then use your hands and the glass to press up the sides of the tin. Chill the crust in the refrigerator while you prepare the filling.

4   Using a stand mixer or large bowl, beat the cream cheese until smooth on low-medium speed. Add the sugar and continue to mix, ensuring you scrape down the sides. Add the eggs one at a time, beating well after each addition. It's crucial that you scrape the bowl at every step to ensure you have a smooth and creamy filling. Add the cream, vanilla, orange flavouring and ginger. Mix until just combined.

continued overleaf

5   Pour the cheesecake filling over the chilled biscuit crust. Place the cheesecake tin in a larger roasting tin or baking dish. Carefully pour hot water into the larger tin, filling it halfway up the sides of the cheesecake tin, creating a hot water bath.

6   Bake the cheesecake for 1 hour–1 hour 10 minutes, or until the cheesecake is set around the edges and only slightly jiggly in the centre. **Check the cheesecake at the 1-hour mark and every 5 minutes after that.**

7   Once the cheesecake is baked, turn off the oven and leave the cheesecake inside, but crack open the door. This will prevent a sudden temperature change, which can cause your cheesecake to crack. Remove after 30 minutes and allow to reach room temperature before chilling for at least 4 hours, overnight is best though.

8   To make the glaze, heat the guava jam in a small saucepan over low heat. Then add the apple juice and lime juice and stir until the mixture is smooth and combined. Do not boil.

9   Allow the glaze to cool for a few minutes, then pour over the top of the cheesecake and chill for 30 minutes before serving!

QUICK FOOLPROOF SALTED CARAMEL

MAKES 1 JAM JAR

225 g (8 oz) granulated sugar
200 ml (7 fl oz) warm double
 (heavy) cream
½ teaspoon flaky salt

I COULD GENUINELY EAT A JAR OF THIS ON ITS OWN. It's so easy to make and completely beats anything you can buy. It's delicious, indulgent and balanced with the flaky salt.

This is definitely a dessert recipe everyone should know because it can be used in a variety of ways, from drizzling it over warm apple crumble cake (see page 184) or ice cream, to using it as a filling for cakes and pastries. Making salted caramel at home is surprisingly simple and requires only a handful of ingredients. The key to achieving the perfect balance of sweetness and saltiness is to use high–quality sea salt and to let the caramel cook until it reaches a deep amber colour. Once you've mastered the basics of the recipe, you can experiment with different flavva variations, such as adding vanilla or spices like cinnamon or nutmeg. Get ready to enjoy the rich and buttery goodness of homemade salted caramel!

1   Add the sugar to a dry high-sided, heavy-bottomed pot over medium–high heat, but don't touch it. Once it starts to melt at the sides and bottom (this should take 2–4 minutes), then check the bottom has also melted with a silicone spatula. If it has, you can then begin to stir the sugar until it turns a deep amber colour. There should be no bubbling – if you get slight bubbling, drop the heat down! Be very careful not to burn the sugar, as it can turn bitter quickly. Be careful not to burn yourself, as a caramel burn isn't what you want.

2   Remove from the heat once melted and immediately add the warm cream to the pan. Be careful, as the mixture will bubble up and steam. Once the bubbling calms down, stir and add the salt. Leave to cool and place into a sterilised jar. This will keep for at least 6 months if stored in a cool, dry place.

NUTMEG ICE CREAM

SERVES 6

Equipment
thermometer
ice-cream machine (optional)
strainer/sieve
2-litre (70-fl oz) ice-cream tub or
    23 x 13 cm (9 x 5 inch) loaf tin

Ice-cream machine method
1 vanilla pod or 2 teaspoons vanilla
    bean paste or extract
700 ml (24 fl oz) full-fat milk
500 ml (17 fl oz) double (heavy)
    cream
2 tablespoons freshly grated nutmeg
½ teaspoon salt
8 egg yolks, at room temperature
220 g (7¾ oz) caster (superfine)
    sugar
½ teaspoon xanthan gum (optional)

No-churn method
400 g (14 oz) can sweetened
    condensed milk
1 teaspoon vanilla extract or vanilla
    bean paste
1 tablespoon freshly grated nutmeg
pinch of salt
600 ml (21 fl oz) cold double
    (heavy) cream

OH MY DAYS, WHERE DO I START?! I never really thought desserts were my speciality, as I'm more of a savoury person, so for that reason alone I really have to make sure that when I make a dessert it hits the spot, and this ice cream hits all the right places.

Funnily enough, I worked in an ice-cream shack one summer when I was sixteen and learned a thing or two. I've also been lucky enough to have had the pleasure of making litres of ice cream every other day when I used to chef it up. I really used to hate that task but it was a blessing in disguise because I learned what could go wrong and how to prevent that. Now, I don't like to toot my own horn too often, but put it this way — I've not had store-bought ice cream for a while because my recipe is that good. The key to amazing ice cream that rivals the store-bought stuff is stabilisers, but don't be scared. This isn't some crazy sciencey stuff, it's just the truth. I use xanthan gum, but really and truly I'm just a perfectionist because the recipe bangs with or without it.

I've included a no-churn method, because not everyone has the luxury of or wants to buy an ice-cream machine. Sometimes it's just a treat every now and then and I completely get that!

ICE-CREAM MACHINE METHOD

1   Alright, so the first thing you want to do is to split your vanilla pod (if using) down the middle with a knife and scrape out the seeds. Save the pod though, that's extra flayva!

2   Then, in a medium pot, add the milk, cream, vanilla seeds and the pod, along with the nutmeg and salt. Heat over medium heat. Don't bring it to the boil, as you want the mixture to be hot but not boiling.

3   Kill the heat and let it steep for 45 minutes, this will allow the vanilla and nutmeg to really infuse the milk.

4   After 40 minutes, make an ice bath by filling a large bowl with ice-cold water and place a small bowl on top of the ice bath. Pop this to the side as you'll need it in a moment. It's just good to be prepared and not scrambling around, you know?

5   Next, place the egg yolks into a bowl along with the sugar. Whisk for 2–3 minutes until the eggs and sugar are combined and pale.

6   At this point your milk has been infused but it will still be hot, so we want to temper our eggs to ensure they don't scramble. Add a ladle of milk into the egg and sugar mixture and whisk. Continue to add half the milk, a ladle at a time.

continued overleaf

7 Now add the tempered eggs back into the remaining milk in the pot and gently bring up the temperature over medium heat. Continuously stir, but do NOT boil the mixture. Once you reach 75–77°C (167°F) pull from the heat.

8 Continue to stir and allow the mixture to drop to 52–55°C (126–131°F), then add the xanthan gum (if using) and use a stick blender to combine. Blend for 2 minutes – after 2 minutes the mixture should have slightly thickened. Strain your custard directly into the small bowl of your ice bath. Stir until it has completely cooled. If using xanthan gum, allow it to chill for 8 hours before moving on to the last step.

9 Lastly, add the ice-cream base to the ice-cream machine and churn according to the manufacturer's directions – it can vary between 30 minutes to over 1 hour.

10 Once it's done, pour into ice-cream containers and freeze for a few hours or overnight before serving. Always let your ice cream sit and thaw for 10–15 minutes before scooping.

NO-CHURN METHOD

1 Place a 23 x 13 cm (9 x 5 inch) loaf tin in the freezer – this massively helps with the process. Everything for this method needs to be chilled.

2 In a bowl, whisk together the condensed milk, vanilla, nutmeg and salt. Pop in the refrigerator until needed.

3 Now, preferably using an electric whisk, whisk the double cream until stiff peaks appear. It should be thick enough for you to hold it above your head with ease – don't do that, but you get what I mean.

4 Grab the condensed milk mixture and slowly add the whipped cream by folding it in. FOLD, not WHISK. We don't want to knock all the air out.

5 Once combined and no streaks remain, grab your freezing-cold loaf tin and smooth in your ice-cream mixture.

6 Cover with cling film (plastic wrap) and freeze for at least 5 hours, but preferably overnight. Allow the ice cream to thaw for 10–15 minutes before scooping and serving.

COCONUT CUSTARD

SERVES 4

600 ml (21 fl oz) tinned coconut milk (mixed)
100 ml (3½ fl oz) double (heavy) cream
2 teaspoons vanilla bean paste or extract
½ teaspoon coconut flavouring
5 egg yolks
8 tablespoons caster (superfine) sugar
4 teaspoons cornflour (cornstarch)
pinch of salt

This coconut custard recipe is the perfect dessert for anyone looking for an easy yet delicious treat. The texture is smooth, creamy and just a lil dreamy. For me it's got just the right amount of sweetness to satisfy my sweet tooth that likes to come out and show itself every now and then. The coconut is a great addition and really adds a tropical twist that you know I love.

You can enjoy this one on its own or with your puddings. You can even mix it with whipped cream and add it to cakes, doughnuts or whatever sweet treats call for something with a coconut twist. This coconut custard is sure to become a favourite amongst dessert lovers everywhere. It's a proper winner in my eyes.

1   In a medium pot, combine the coconut milk (make sure you've shaken the tin), cream, vanilla and coconut flavouring. Slowly simmer over low heat until hot.

2   Whisk the egg yolks, sugar and cornflour together in a bowl until smooth and combined.

3   Pour the infused hot milk and cream mixture onto your sugar and eggs, whisking constantly to avoid lumps or clumping.

4   Then put it back into the pan. Gently heat over low heat, add the salt (it brings out the sweetness) and whisk until the custard starts to thicken and can coat the back of a spoon easily. To ensure there's no lumps, strain your custard using a sieve.

5   Serve immediately or allow to cool with cling film (plastic wrap) touching the surface. This stops a film from forming, which I hate!

RUM PUNCH

GUINNESS PUNCH

SERVES 6–8

400 ml (14 fl oz) fresh pineapple juice
400 ml (14 fl oz) fresh mango juice or tropical juice
400 ml (14 fl oz) fresh orange juice
200 ml (7 fl oz) fresh lime juice
300 ml (10½ fl oz) grenadine or strawberry syrup
250 ml (9 fl oz) white rum
250 ml (9 fl oz) coconut rum
¼ teaspoon freshly grated nutmeg
1 orange, sliced
plenty of ice, to serve

This rum punch is a recipe very close to my heart and I'm telling you it's a sip of sunshine. It never disappoints and it's perfect for wowing family and friends or impressing at a gathering. Take it easy though, I beg.

The thing I love about rum punch is that the recipe isn't set in stone and you can mix it up and tailor it to your liking. In my recipe I like to use a strong white rum and coconut rum to really provide tropical flayvas; however, if you prefer a dark rum or a spiced rum, then you can easily substitute them. No two people make rum punch the same and over time you'll figure out your rum punch palate. This recipe is super quick to make and simple — it doesn't take a lot of time but it's guaranteed FLAYVAS!

1   First, combine all the ingredients, except the orange slices, in a large bowl or jug and stir together.

2   Then add the orange slices. At this point you can leave your rum punch to chill until ready to serve.

3   Serve over lots of ice and enjoy responsibly!

SERVES 6–8 (DOUBLE OR TRIPLE THE BATCH IF NEEDED)

550 ml (19 fl oz) Guinness
400 g (14 oz) can condensed milk
400 ml (14 fl oz) vanilla Nurishment
1 teaspoon freshly grated nutmeg
1 teaspoon vanilla extract
100 ml (3½ fl oz) white rum (optional but recommended)
ice, to serve

Jamaican Guinness punch is a traditional and beloved beverage that takes me down memory lane. It is perfect for Sunday dinners and is always present at any family gathering. It's ideal for when you want to enjoy a sweet, creamy and addictive drink. Easy to make, this recipe will give you the best-tasting Guinness punch you've ever had. I have very fond memories of begging my nana to let me have some and I was always told no because it contains alcohol. Eventually I got to a certain age where I was allowed a tiny glass with my Sunday dinner. The only way to describe this is that it's like a Jamaican adult milkshake, but better.

Guinness punch dates back to the early 1900s when Guinness was first introduced to Jamaica. It quickly became a popular drink amongst the masses. Today, it is a staple in Jamaican cuisine and is enjoyed by most households. One thing Jamaican people will do is make a punch and be sure to make it damn well! Go ahead and try this recipe for a taste of Jamaica at home.

1   In a blender or very large bowl, mix together the Guinness, condensed milk, vanilla Nurishment, nutmeg and vanilla. Mix until combined. I like my punch quite sweet; however, I recommend starting with half the amount of condensed milk listed and adjusting to suit your own taste buds.

2   Add the white rum if you like – I'm Jamaican, so I'm always in the mood for a likkle rum!

3   Cover and chill for at least 30 minutes. Once chilled, give the punch a quick stir to combine any settled ingredients. Fill glasses with ice and pour over the Guinness punch.

4   Serve and enjoy responsibly.

MANGO LYCHEE MINT MOJITO

MAKES 6

180 ml (6 fl oz) mango purée, or
 1 large ripe mango, puréed
36 fresh mint leaves (6 per drink),
 plus extra to garnish
2 limes, cut into wedges, plus extra
 to serve
150–300 ml (5–10½ fl oz) white rum
300 ml (10½ fl oz) lychee juice
1–2 tablespoons simple syrup
 per drink
ice
soda or sparkling water

Simple syrup
150 g (5½ oz) granulated sugar
150 ml (5 fl oz) water

A fruity, tropical, and refreshing cocktail that's easy to make and absolutely tasty? I've got you. This delightful twist on the classic mojito features the sweet and juicy flavvas of fresh mango and lychee, which are perfectly complemented by the crisp freshness of mint and the tangy kick of lime.

For this recipe you can use tinned mango pulp or make your own with fresh mango.

I use a simple syrup to add some sweetness but it's not essential; you can sweeten this with agave, but it's cheaper just to make a syrup. Regardless of what you choose, this mojito is sure to be a hit at your next party, gathering or just on a summer's day.

1   Begin by preparing the simple syrup, which is simple... In a small pot, combine the sugar and water. Bring to the boil, stir and allow the sugar to dissolve. Once boiling, simmer for 2 minutes and place straight into a sterilised jar. This will keep refrigerated for up to 6 months.

2   I use tinned mango purée but you can make it yourself by blending fresh mango. Peel and remove the flesh from around the seed (discard the seed, but of course you have to eat the remaining flesh off!). Blend until smooth.

3   In a tall glass, add 6 mint leaves and 2 lime wedges. Use a muddler or the back of a spoon to gently crush the ingredients together, releasing the mint oils and lime juice.

4   Add 2 tablespoons of mango purée, 25 ml (5 teaspoons) white rum for a single and 50 ml (3½ tablespoons) for a double, along with 50 ml (3½ tablespoons) lychee juice and 1 tablespoon of simple syrup. Mix and stir until combined. Add ice cubes to the glass, filling it about two-thirds full.

5   Top with soda or sparkling water. If your drink isn't sweet enough, add another tablespoon of simple syrup. Gently stir and garnish with mint and fresh lime wedges.

All recipes photographed on previous spread

SPIC
&
FLAY

This is a very small collection of some of my favourite ways to add spice and flayva into my recipes. Now, I've tried to keep these all very simple because it's not easy making dry seasonings at home, especially if you don't have a dehydrator, so I've tried to keep this as inclusive as possible, while still delivering on flayva. Most of these are absolute staples that I can't live without and I think you'll find that too. They're the basics, but without them many of my recipes simply aren't possible. Like I always say though, flayvas are unique and individual to each person, so this section is really where you build and develop the flayva profiles that you like.

GREEN SEASONING

1 green bell pepper (capsicum),
   cored and deseeded
½ onion
35 g (1¼ oz) fresh flat-leaf parsley
35 g (1¼ oz) fresh coriander
   (cilantro)
35 g (1¼ oz) fresh basil leaves
6 garlic cloves
5 sprigs of fresh thyme
3 spring onions (scallions)
1 rib of celery
½ Scotch bonnet pepper
½ teaspoon pimento (allspice)
   berries
1 teaspoon salt
2 tablespoons olive oil

Made from a blend of the freshest aromatic herbs, this paste here is a staple in Caribbean cooking. **There's different variations amongst different islands but the core ingredients always remain the same. No stew dish is complete without it, it's a flayva bomb! It's also known as sofrito in the Dominican Republic or epis in Haitian cooking. Whatever you know it as, you know it's the real deal.**

The great thing about this seasoning is that it can be frozen for up to 3–6 months, yet still packs a punch. It's great for meat, sauces, fish or adding as a base to marinades. More often than not, if I'm cooking a curry or stew, I'll bang a frozen cube or two in while it's bubbling away. I use this recipe a lot and it really does elevate the flayvas, so it would have been rude not to share it with you.

1   Place all the ingredients in a blender. Blitz until a smooth paste has formed. It should resemble the consistency of a very thick smoothie.

2   Keep refrigerated in an airtight container for up to a week. You can also place the mixture into ice-cube moulds, freeze and pop out of the moulds into a container and have little green seasoning cubes on hand. This is what I do!

LEMON PEPPER SEASONING

MAKES 1 SMALL JAM JAR

8 large unwaxed lemons
3 tablespoons black pepper
1½ tablespoons onion powder
1 tablespoon garlic powder
1 tablespoon salt

A staple to up your cooking game, but an easy one that's honestly foolproof. **I feel like lemon pepper seasoning is massively underrated where I'm from and can really level up your midweek meals. It's probably something I use once or twice a week. It's a great way to elevate something simple like salmon, chicken, wings and vegetables and you wouldn't believe that something with only five ingredients could make your food taste so great, but it's all about the balance of ingredients.**

Now, believe it or not, most lemons in the supermarket are waxed and that's unpleasant for anything that you're consuming. It won't kill you to eat it but I'm trying to teach you guys the right ways to get the best results. So please try to buy unwaxed lemons for this one. **If you can't get hold of unwaxed lemons, then simply soak your lemons in hot water for a minute or two and wipe away the wax using kitchen paper.**

Now, you don't need a dehydrator to make this seasoning, as lemon zest is so fine that it will easily dehydrate in the oven or left in a cool, dry space in your kitchen for a few days. That may seem a long time, but it's a pretty minimal-effort task.

1   Preheat your oven to its lowest setting – most ovens range from about 30–75°C (85–165°F). The higher the temperature, the quicker the zest will dehydrate, but it will be darker.

2   Remove the zest of your lemons with a zester and place onto a baking tray lined with baking parchment. Bake for 30 minutes–1 hour. Alternatively, you can dehydrate at 50°C (122°F) for 45 minutes.

3   Once cooled, combine the lemon zest in a bowl with all the remaining ingredients.

4   Store in an airtight container and use within 6 months – I doubt it will last that long though!

CHILLI OIL

MAKES 2 JAM JARS

50 g (1¾ oz) dried Chinese chillies
   or 5 tablespoons chilli flakes
2 tablespoons chilli flakes (only
   add extra chilli flakes if using
   Chinese chillies)
4 star anise
1 cinnamon stick
1 teaspoon ground Sichuan
   peppercorns
1 tablespoon minced fresh ginger
2 tablespoons minced garlic
1 teaspoon MSG (optional)
2 tablespoons dark soy sauce
1 tablespoon toasted sesame oil
8 garlic cloves, thinly sliced
1 shallot, thinly sliced
500 ml (17 fl oz) vegetable oil

CHILLI OIL, CHILLI, CHILLI, CHILLI, OIL. Where do we start? I add it to most meals. If you're into spice, then you need this one. Add it to eggs, rice, noodles, pasta...

The great thing about this recipe is it's so adaptable, but what I will say is Sichuan peppercorns aren't for everyone! They have a slight numbing effect if you're not used to them. Now, dried Chinese chillies really take this up to the next level. You can easily just use regular chilli flakes in this recipe and it will still taste amazing but I'm just sharing the knowledge, you know?

When making the crispy shallots and garlic, it's key that you use a deep, small, heavy-bottomed pot. Secondly, infuse the oil slowly with a gradual increase in heat. Now, depending on your heat source, you may need a high heat. If you're using gas, you can work with a medium–high heat. If you're using anything else, you'll need a high heat. This creates the perfect conditions to get them nice, golden, crispy and not burnt! Lastly, you have to keep stirring — don't take your eyes off them because they will burn! Make sure you remove them before they reach a golden colour, as they will continue to cook afterwards.

1   So the first thing you want to do is blitz the Chinese chillies in a food processor or blender. You want the mixture to still be quite coarse and resemble the consistency of actual chilli flakes...you know the ones you buy from the supermarket with the seeds?

2   In a heatproof bowl, combine the chillies with the remaining ingredients, except the sliced garlic, shallot and oil. Pop the chilli mix to the side with a sieve on top until time to infuse.

3   Place the sliced garlic and shallot in a pot and cover with the oil. Then start over low heat and gradually work your way up to medium–high heat over the course of 3 minutes. Once it starts to bubble, keep stirring regularly for a few minutes, or until the shallot and garlic are lightly golden. They will continue to cook, so pull them out before they reach that perfect golden colour.

4   Carefully pour the oil directly into the sieve sitting on top of the bowl. Remove the sieve and allow the shallot and garlic to cool while you combine the oil with your chilli mixture. I like to use my hands to lightly crush the shallot and garlic mixture before placing it into the chilli oil.

5   Store in airtight sterilised jars for 2–3 months.

MANGO HOT SAUCE

400 g (14 oz) red chillies, such as
   jalapeño, Fresno or large red
   Thai chillies
3 Scotch bonnet peppers
2 ripe mangoes (roughly 350 g/
   12 oz), peeled and sliced into strips
4 cm (1½ inch) thumb of fresh ginger,
   peeled and sliced
1 onion, diced
1 large bulb of garlic, cloves
   separated and peeled, plus
   2 garlic cloves, roughly chopped
1.5 litres (52 fl oz) cold water
3 tablespoons, plus 1 teaspoon salt
1 carrot, peeled and sliced
½ teaspoon flaky salt
250 ml (9 fl oz) vegetable oil
   (enough for the Scotch
   bonnet, carrots and garlic
   to be submerged)
¼ teaspoon ground cumin
½ teaspoon ground allspice
125 ml (4 fl oz) rice wine vinegar
   or distilled vinegar
125 ml (4 fl oz) water
2 tablespoons honey
½ teaspoon xanthan gum (optional)

NOW THIS HOT SAUCE IS A LITTLE 'FANCY', BUT FANTASTIC AND WORTH THE EXTRA STEPS. **The wonderful thing about hot sauce is that you don't need loads of it and because the chillies are fermented it means the shelf life is a lot longer. I said this recipe is fancy, but in reality, it's not because there's any out-of-this-world techniques. You literally bang your chillies in a jar and brine them for a week.**

This recipe is so special because I can't live without hot sauce. It's funny because I don't really like spicy food, but pops of spice? That's what makes my heart sing. It should be apparent by now that I love a sweet and spicy mix. Now, the mango in this hot sauce isn't necessarily sweet like that. The sweetness is subtle, but noticeable.

Fermentation is really easy, the most important thing is ensuring that your jar is sterile; **if it isn't you end up with a funky mess. One thing to note when fermenting is that cloudiness in the liquid is not alarming, but mould or fuzz is bad. Mould isn't the end of the world if a small spot appears, but if it reappears you need to start again and ensure your jars are clean. There are so many variables that can impact fermentation. It's absolutely key that your chillies are submerged, which is why you want to place a small ramekin or glass weight on top of your chillies. If you get any seeds floating, remove them from the surface before storing to ferment. Lastly, it's optional but really worth it if you care for the small details. Adding a very, very small amount of xanthan gum will help to emulsify the sauce and create a really nice creamy texture.**

1   Alright, so the first thing you want to do is rinse all of your fresh produce and pat dry. Slice the tops off your chillies and pierce two of the Scotch bonnet peppers, then slice them lengthways to expose the seeds, or in rings. I like to keep the seeds as this is a hot sauce after all, but it's not uncommon to remove them. Place them into a 2-litre (70-fl oz) sterilised jar along with the mangoes, ginger, onion and roughly chopped garlic.

2   In a bowl, combine the cold water and salt, stir until the salt is dissolved and pour over your chilli and mango mix. Keep the chillies submerged with a ramekin or heavy object and close the jar. You can even scrunch up some baking parchment to keep them down.

3   Now don't be scared, you're going to let this sit for 5–10 days in a cool, dark place. The time you let this ferment for will vary depending on the environment and time of year. If you're making this in summer

continued overleaf

or your location is quite warm, then it's most likely that your chillies will only need 5 days. Your chilli mix should reduce in colour and you should see bubbles as the mixture turns acidic and releases air.

4   If you're using a screw-top lid, leave some space as you'll need the air to escape. If you're using a clip-top jar, then you'll want to pop this open once every day to let the air out. Check your chillies every day or so. Cloudy liquid is not alarming.

5   After a few days of fermenting, work on the confit garlic – this will last in the refrigerator for up to a week, so it's great to have it ready beforehand. Preheat the oven to 120°C fan (275°F/Gas mark 1). Add the peeled and separated garlic cloves to a small ovenproof dish along with the carrot, remaining Scotch bonnet pepper and the flaky salt. Cover with enough oil for the ingredients to be submerged. Bake for 1–1½ hours, or until the garlic has softened but gained barely any colour. Strain and reserve 60 ml (4 tablespoons) of oil for later. The remaining oil can be used for cooking.

6   Strain your fermentation liquid, but don't throw it away. Place the fermented goodness into a blender with the strained confit garlic, carrot and Scotch bonnet, along with the cumin, allspice, vinegar, water, honey and 5 tablespoons of fermentation brine liquid.

7   Blend at high speed and slowly stream in the 60 ml (4 tablespoons) reserved oil. Once the oil is in, add the xanthan gum (if using) – this will really thicken the sauce and help it emulsify. At this point you can give it a taste. Not seasoned enough? Add more brine water. Too acidic? Add more cold water. Too spicy? Add more cold water to cut the heat.

8   I like to strain my hot sauce as it just provides a smoother texture, but it's completely optional. Then store, refrigerated, for up to 12 months. Emphasis on refrigerated – remember the sauce is fermented and it will continue to ferment if left out. I don't think you want to crack open your bottle of hot sauce and have it explode all over you.

WET JERK MARINADE

MAKES 2 JAM JARS

2 tablespoons pimento (allspice)
  berries
1 cinnamon stick
1 whole nutmeg
1 teaspoon whole black peppercorns
7 spring onions (scallions)
1 medium onion
2 Scotch bonnet peppers
10 garlic cloves
10 sprigs of fresh thyme
6 dried pimento leaves (optional)
3 dried bay leaves
4 tablespoons dark soft brown sugar
2 tablespoons honey
2 tablespoons white vinegar
2 tablespoons minced fresh ginger
1 tablespoon flaky salt
1 tablespoon ground allspice
1 teaspoon black pepper
5 tablespoons dark soy sauce
4 tablespoons fresh lime juice
4 tablespoons fresh orange juice
3 tablespoons olive oil
2 tablespoons Worcestershire sauce
1 tablespoon browning

JERK MARINADE IS A STAPLE IN CARIBBEAN COOKING, ESPECIALLY JAMAICAN CUISINE. It's definitely a staple in my cooking. It's not something I use just for jerk chicken on a grill. You can use it on fish and veg, or add it to tacos, pasta and sauces. This recipe is super simple and will definitely make you think twice about ever buying pre-made jerk marinade again. The flavours that erupt in your mouth from this marinade are one of a kind and unique to jerk marinade — it can't be compared to anything else.

Jerk marinade is traditionally made with Scotch bonnet peppers; not only do they provide an amazing and intense heat, but they have a really distinct peppery and almost sweet undertone. The next best thing to a Scotch bonnet is the habanero pepper. Now if you can't handle spice, I would suggest deseeding the Scotch bonnet, as the seeds are the true spicy element to the pepper.

The key to the best jerk marinade is FRESH ingredients, that's what really makes the difference and all you need for this recipe is a decent blender and about 10 minutes of your time. Now, there's ingredients like pimento leaves listed, because for me this is how I get as close to the authentic flavvas as possible. It's not the end of the world if you can't get hold of them but, trust me, it makes a difference.

1   The first thing you want to do is toast your pimento berries, cinnamon stick, whole nutmeg and peppercorns in a pan over medium-high heat for a few minutes or until fragrant. By doing this you intensify the flavvas!

2   Now you want to grind your toasted spices until coarse. If you don't have a spice grinder, you can simply add all of these ingredients to the blender, minus the nutmeg. You'll need to grate in the nutmeg before blending.

3   Now add all the remaining ingredients to the blender and blitz until smooth.

4   Transfer to an airtight container and store in the refrigerator for up to 2 weeks. You can also freeze this in cubes and defrost when ready to use; however, it will lose some potency.

DRY JERK RUB

MAKES 1 SMALL JAM JAR

3 tablespoons dried chives
2 tablespoons dried thyme
3 tablespoons pimento (allspice)
  berries
4 tablespoons dark brown
  molasses sugar
2 tablespoons onion powder
2 tablespoons garlic powder
1 tablespoon salt
1 tablespoon ground ginger
1 tablespoon black pepper
2 teaspoons ground cinnamon
2 teaspoons freshly grated nutmeg
2 teaspoons Scotch bonnet chilli
  powder or cayenne pepper
2 teaspoons black pepper

When a lot of people think of jerk seasoning, they automatically think of a fresh wet marinade that you typically slather on chicken and bang on a BBQ to get that jerk flayva that everybody knows. But the wet marinade isn't as versatile when it comes to cooking meats with different methods. For example, if you want a pan-seared chicken with the flayvas of jerk, it wouldn't work that well as it's wet and it would just steam away instead of getting a great sear.

I would like to clarify though; you can't just call anything jerk. The seasoning is one part of this beautifully flavoured food, but the method of cooking really determines if it's jerk. If you put it in the oven? It's not a jerk. Gas grill? Not jerk. Not cooked with pimento wood over a fire? Not jerk. Not to worry though, I'm not the jerk police. While I'll always acknowledge the true and authentic way to make jerk, food is supposed to be accessible and versatile, and that's what this seasoning is for.

This jerk rub is warm, punching with flavour, yet very subtly sweet, with smoky undertones to imitate the flayvas of a grill. The great thing about dry jerk rub is that you can use it for the same cooking methods as the wet marinade, plus baking, frying and searing.

1   Okay, so the dried chives, thyme and pimento berries are whole, so you want to grind these down to a coarse consistency. You don't want them to resemble powder, we're aiming for more like a coffee granule-type consistency.

2   Combine with the remaining ingredients in a bowl and store in an airtight container. This rub will remain potent and fresh for at least 6 months, but I promise you it won't take you long to finish this off!

SEASONED FLOUR

MAKES ENOUGH FOR 5—6
BATCHES OF CHICKEN WINGS

500 g (1 lb 2 oz) plain (all-purpose)
  flour
150 g (5½ oz) cornflour (cornstarch)
60 g (2¼ oz) salt
40 g (1½ oz) all-purpose seasoning
10 g (¼ oz) mustard powder
40 g (1½ oz) dark soft brown sugar
15 g (½ oz) smoked paprika
10 g (¼ oz) cayenne pepper
15 g (½ oz) garlic powder
15 g (½ oz) onion powder
30 g (1 oz) black pepper
15 g (½ oz) dried thyme
15 g (½ oz) ground cumin
10 g (¼ oz) baking powder

People have always asked me for my seasoned flour recipe, especially after seeing my fried chicken. I'd like to say I'm a bit of a fried chicken connoisseur, but that's thanks to my varied chef experience and the fact that even though I didn't have fried chicken often when I was younger, when I did, it hit differently. Over the years I've watched my family and friends make it and I had to find a way to make a crispy coating that was full of flavvas but that actually stuck to the chicken. I don't think there's anything worse than biting into fried chicken and the coating crumbling off and not even making it into your mouth... cue sad music.

The amount of salt might seem alarming and you can reduce it. When I'm using seasoned flour, I'll add very little or no salt to the meat. I'll still go in with herbs and spices so the background flavvas are there but salt is really what makes everything pop. We all have different taste buds, so play with the measurements. You can always use less salt and dust your chicken with extra seasoning if you think it's missing that!

This is my basic seasoned flour, but you can tweak it and add Cajun instead of all-purpose seasoning or add dry jerk rub (see opposite). Cooking is about experimenting and finding what you like. This recipe has never failed me though.

Please note, this is a bulk seasoned flour recipe.

1   Combine all the ingredients in a large bowl. Store in an airtight container and use whenever a recipe calls for it. The shelf life of this is up to 6 months; after that the ground spices start to lose their potency.

HERB SALT

MAKES 1 JAM JAR

200 g (7 oz) flaky salt
10 sprigs of fresh rosemary
4 sprigs of fresh thyme
4 sprigs of fresh sage
4 garlic cloves
zest of ½ lemon

THIS ONE'S PACKED WITH TONS OF FLAYVA and if you're a crispy potato lover and don't have this recipe in your arsenal, then what are you playing at?! Recipes like this are great because a lot of people think you require crazy skills to make this bright green herbaceous salt, but you don't and it's so customisable. If there's a certain herb you don't like, then swap it out for one you do or double up on the rosemary. You want to use a flaky salt, not because it's fancy but because if you use a salt that's fine, when you grind it down the consistency will resemble powder, which isn't what we're aiming for. If you're like my nana and like spice with everything, then you can simply add chilli powder to give it that kick. Remember, cooking is about finding what works for you; every single recipe in this book is adaptable.

I've selected these herbs because they all complement each other really, really well, and they complement protein and veg ridiculously well. Roast potatoes are one of my favourites and everyone knows I love to elevate a roastie where I can, and this salt does that. You can even use it to zhuzh up broccoli, all you need to do is toss your cooked broccoli in a pan with a lil butter and a sprinkle of rosemary salt. These little tweaks are what take food to the next level and ultimately make it an experience and not something you just eat for survival.

1   Add the salt to a spice grinder or food processor.

2   Remove the rosemary leaves from the stem by holding the end of the stem and pulling the rosemary in the opposite direction to which the leaves grow. Repeat this step with the thyme too.

3   Roughly chop the sage leaves and mince the garlic and lemon zest together.

4   Add all the ingredients to your grinder or processor and blitz for 30 seconds–1 minute, checking the consistency after 30 seconds. Pulse for 5–10 seconds until all the ingredients are broken down. At this point you should smell the herbs in the air!

5   Use to sprinkle over chips, lamb, steak or anything that requires some herby love! Store in an airtight container in a cool, dry place for up to 6 months.

SCOTCH BONNET HONEY SAUCE

MAKES 1 JAM JAR

½–1 Scotch bonnet pepper (you can remove or reduce the seeds to control the spice if you like)
350 g (12 oz) thick mayonnaise
1 teaspoon smoked paprika
½ teaspoon black pepper
3 fresh basil leaves
1 garlic clove, minced
4 tablespoons ketchup
3 tablespoons honey or agave syrup

I think this is probably my go-to/most used sauce when it comes to savoury dishes. **If I'm not using it as a dip, then I'll definitely use it as a base for another sauce. It's just too good. The great thing is you can really control the spice with this one, and if you want the taste of chillies without the blow-your-head-off heat, then simply ditch the seeds. I like to use ½ Scotch bonnet pepper with the seeds, as it's the perfect level of spice for me.**

This recipe is very, very easily made vegan. **We're lucky to live in a time where vegan mayo is available in every major supermarket. So simply use vegan mayo instead and agave to bring in the sweetness. I promise it'll taste just as good.**

1   Bang all the ingredients in a blender, except the honey, and blitz until smooth.

2   Stir in half the honey and give it a taste, then adjust the sweetness accordingly. I personally use all of it because you guys know I love honey by now.

3   This will keep in an airtight container in the refrigerator for 1 week.

HOT HONEY

600 g (1 lb 5 oz) honey
6–10 dried habanero chillies or
  Scotch bonnet peppers
6–8 chile de arbol
2 tablespoons cayenne pepper
1 tablespoon chilli flakes

WHEW, CHILLI–INFUSED HONEY? My oh my, this one's going to take your cooking to the next level. I use this every single week without fail. I created this chilli–infused honey for my fried chicken because sweet, savoury and spicy is my favourite combo. Anyone that knows me knows I'm honey mad; I feel like by now you'll have caught onto this. Now, this recipe is so simple and it's so customisable because you can use your favourite chillies — just adjust the spice or tone it down. The world really is your oyster with this one.

For best results, you really want to use good–quality honey and dried chillies. This recipe still works with fresh chillies, but because they contain water and the moisture hasn't been removed from them this impacts the consistency of the honey and also shortens the shelf life, which means you will have to keep this refrigerated and it will last for up to a week.

I use Mexican chile de arbol and dried habanero chillies, but you can use dried Thai chillies or chilli powders like cayenne pepper, standard chilli powder or Scotch bonnet chilli powder for some real kick!

1   Bang all the ingredients into a pot, stir and simmer for 30 minutes over the lowest heat. You don't want your honey to boil at all, we just want to gently heat and infuse the honey.

2   Strain and allow it to cool before using.

3   If you use dried ingredients, your honey will last for about 2 years. Honey has no expiry date, unlike most food products, and will last indefinitely. The chillies and powders will have an expiration date of 2–3 years but if I'm being honest, it never lasts past 4 months because it's that good.

PINEAPPLE PEPPER JAM

MAKES 1 JAM JAR

1–2 Scotch bonnet peppers
  (with seeds for spice)
1 red bell pepper (capsicum)
500 g (1 lb 2 oz) fresh or tinned
  pineapple, finely diced
juice of 1 lime
2 tablespoons apple cider vinegar
300 g (10½ oz) caster (superfine)
  sugar
¼ teaspoon ground cinnamon
pinch of salt
1–3 tablespoons water (optional)

It's sweet, it's sticky, it spices up sandwiches and burgers, you can have it with toasted pitta or you can mix it up and add it to your marinades for a spicy but sweet kick. This jam is serious and the possibilities are endless when you think of this jam as a tropical chutney.

For me, the whole purpose of this jam is to be spicy — it's a chilli jam after all! Scotch bonnet peppers will vary in heat depending on size, freshness and colour. I always start off with one Scotch bonnet and, once all the ingredients are in the pot, I'll taste test and see if it needs more spice. If it does, I'll add half a minced Scotch bonnet without the seeds and keep working my way up until it's just right.

I prefer using fresh pineapple over tinned pineapple for this recipe but it's not the end of the world if you use tinned!

1   This one is easy-peasy, my people. Blend the Scotch bonnet and red pepper together; the mixture does not need to be smooth, you just don't want huge chunks.

2   Add the blended pepper mixture to a medium pot along with the pineapple, lime juice, apple cider vinegar, sugar, cinnamon and salt. The salt really brings out the sweetness, so don't skip this step.

3   Bring the mixture to the boil and, once boiling, drop the heat to low and let it simmer away and reduce for 45 minutes, or until the pineapple starts to soften. Now, there should still be some sauce in the pan at the end, and as this cools it will thicken. If it's already super thick at this point, it's not the end of the world, you'll just have a thick jam. To loosen it, add the water as needed.

4   Allow your jam to cool before transferring to clean and sterilised jars. This will keep in the refrigerator for 4–6 weeks, but will it last that long? Find out in the next episode.

RUM & GINGER BEER BBQ SAUCE

MAKES 1 LARGE JAR

2 teaspoons vegetable oil
3 tablespoons minced fresh ginger
1 tablespoon minced garlic
½ onion, diced
6 tablespoons dark muscovado
  sugar
125 ml (4 fl oz) white rum
400 ml (14 fl oz) ginger beer
300 g (10½ oz) ketchup
1 tablespoon fresh lime juice
1 tablespoon apple cider vinegar
1 tablespoon Worcestershire sauce
3 tablespoons honey
3 tablespoons molasses or
  2 tablespoons black treacle

BBQ sauce is great, but you know if I can elevate something or add my own little twist, then I absolutely will and that's exactly what I did. It's slightly sweet, sticky and goes so well with ribs, wings, chicken or even as a dipping sauce. It's pretty straightforward to make, but the addition of ginger really adds a subtle aromatic kick.

Now, I'm an island boy at heart and I'd like to say I can handle my drink. I use a 63% white rum for this recipe and it does the trick. You may need to increase the amount of rum by a shot or two if you're using a weaker rum.

1   So, the first thing you want to do is add the oil to a pan over medium heat, then add the ginger, garlic and onion. Sauté over medium heat until your onion starts to soften and become translucent.

2   Add the dark muscovado sugar and stir until it begins to bubble and turn a light brown caramel colour.

3   Deglaze the pan with 75 ml (2½ fl oz) of the white rum and cook for 5 minutes over medium heat.

4   Then add the ginger beer, ketchup, lime juice, vinegar, Worcestershire sauce, honey and molasses. **At this point it will be very liquidy and that's fine, don't panic.** Allow to reduce and simmer over medium heat for 10–15 minutes, or until you reach your desired consistency for a sauce. Just remember it will thicken slightly as it cools.

5   Once thickened, add the remaining rum and you're done. This is completely optional, but I don't like lots of chunky bits in my sauces, so I like to strain my sauce and add a few dollops of the chunks back in for a little texture and flayva pop. Store in a sterilised jar for up to 2 weeks and keep refrigerated.

INDEX

ACKNOWLEDGEMENTS

Flayvaful, what a journey it's been, a true labour of bloody love. A few breakdowns later and a little self-doubt... We did it. A published author? I made it! It doesn't seem like enough and it probably never will be but THANK YOU. It's funny because I never dreamed of this being my career and I certainly never thought I would be publishing a book in my lifetime. To the people that support me, you reading this book – thank you. The confidence and drive that has been poured into me isn't something I take lightly. Every day I'm trying to do better and be better so I can do what I do best, which is create wonderful recipes and share the joy of cooking. I can't even say I'm living my wildest dreams because even my wildest dreams didn't even stretch this far.

This all started in lockdown, from posting videos because I desperately wanted to be a chef yet didn't have enough experience to be taken seriously by anyone. I wanted to create a catalogue of recipes to show potential employers, but little did I know I was forging my own career.

To my nana, thank you for creating and injecting so many core memories into my life that have created such a beautiful foundation for my journey with food. Thank you for always trusting the process, even when that meant me throwing in the towel for jobs some would have been so grateful to have, but they just never aligned with my spirit. Thank you for being the amazing woman that you are. The love I have for you is unmatched. I have so many fond memories of you making breakfast on Saturday mornings. Thank you for letting me lick the cake bowl when we would make cakes!! Thank you for loving me unconditionally and allowing me to pursue what I wanted to do, even if it didn't make sense to you. I remember when I told you I was a chef and you were so proud of me.

To my siblings, Reece, Isaiah and Soraya, I love you guys so much. Thank you for allowing me to be your big brother. Everyone sees the great food now but you guys really lived through it all. You experienced when I was so bad at making rice it would turn out stodgy like mash potato, haha!! Everything I do is to make all you guys proud. Making you proud is priceless and I hope I can one day repay you all for the patience you've had with me. You've always believed in me and I wouldn't change our journey. A special thank you to my little sister, my biggest critic. I wouldn't have it any other way.

To my wonderful lady and best friend in one. Thank you for putting up with my sleepless nights, working until silly am testing recipes. Thank you for being my devoted taste tester, though I think you should be thanking me for that role, because I'm sure there's people out there ready to risk it all to try my food and you get it on tap. Thank you for keeping me calm, you really saw the good, the bad and the ugly, yet always pushed me to keep going, even when it wasn't going right, you always found a way to keep me grounded.

To my best friends Arleene and Canchez, thank you for checking that I'm still alive throughout this whole process! Canchez, my brother. Thank you for being my darg and always letting me know how proud you are of me. You've really seen the journey and we've somehow not killed each other... Arleene, thank you from the bottom of my heart. There's no Grubworks Kitchen without you, I told you my ideas and you always rooted for me, you really believed in my talent and took the time to nurture me. You're more than a friend, you're family, forever.

To my management team, Ange, Alan and Heather, thank you for believing in me and checking in on me every step of the way. A really big thank you to Ange, I wouldn't be where I am if it wasn't for you. I remember our first meeting; you made me realise my value and that the world is really my oyster. Whenever I'm in doubt I think back to that moment with you and Alan. There's still so much work for me to do and this is only the beginning for us!

Thank you to my wonderful publishing team at Murdoch books, especially Céline. Thank you for seeing the vision when *Flayvaful* was nothing but an idea and a big dream. Thank you to Jo and Lauren from my agency, you really saw *Flayvaful* before it was a *Flayvaful* and was simply just a hot mess that you guys somehow helped turn into magic!

Lastly, to my grandparents, Granny and Grandad. Where would I be without you guys? I guess it all really started with you two. Grandad, oh how I miss you and your cheeky ways, I still make my tea and keep the teabag in, just like you did. I will always cherish the times we spent in the garden together. You were a man of few words, but they all had impact. Granny, I miss you and your stories, I miss watching WWE wrestling with you (I'm sorry, but my granny was the coolest, are you mad?). You never got to see The Grubworks Kitchen take off, but I hope I've made you both proud.

Published in 2024 by Murdoch Books,
an imprint of Allen & Unwin

Murdoch Books UK
Ormond House
26–27 Boswell Street
London WC1N 3JZ
Phone: +44 (0) 20 8785 5995
murdochbooks.co.uk
info@murdochbooks.co.uk

Murdoch Books Australia
Cammeraygal Country
83 Alexander Street
Crows Nest NSW 2065
Phone: +61 (0)2 8425 0100
murdochbooks.com.au
info@murdochbooks.com.au

For corporate orders and custom publishing,
contact our business development team at
salesenquiries@murdochbooks.com.au

Publisher: Céline Hughes
Project Editor: Vicky Orchard
Art Direction & Design: Nikki Ellis
Photographer: Steven Joyce
Prop Stylist: Faye Wears-Logue
Food Stylist: Lizzie Harris
Production Director, UK: Niccolò De Bianchi
Production Director, Australia: Lou Playfair

ISBN 978 1922616821

A catalogue record for this book is available
from the British Library

Colour reproduction by Born Group, London, UK
Printed by 1010 Printing International Ltd., China

OVEN GUIDE: You may find cooking times vary
depending on the oven you are using. The recipes
in this book are based on fan-assisted oven
temperatures. For non-fan-assisted ovens, as a
general rule, set the oven temperature to 20°C (35°F)
higher than indicated in the recipe.

TABLESPOON MEASURES: We have used 15 ml
(3 teaspoon) tablespoon measures.

10 9 8 7 6 5 4 3 2 1

A catalogue record for this
book is available from the
National Library of Australia